50 Nifty Beaded Cards

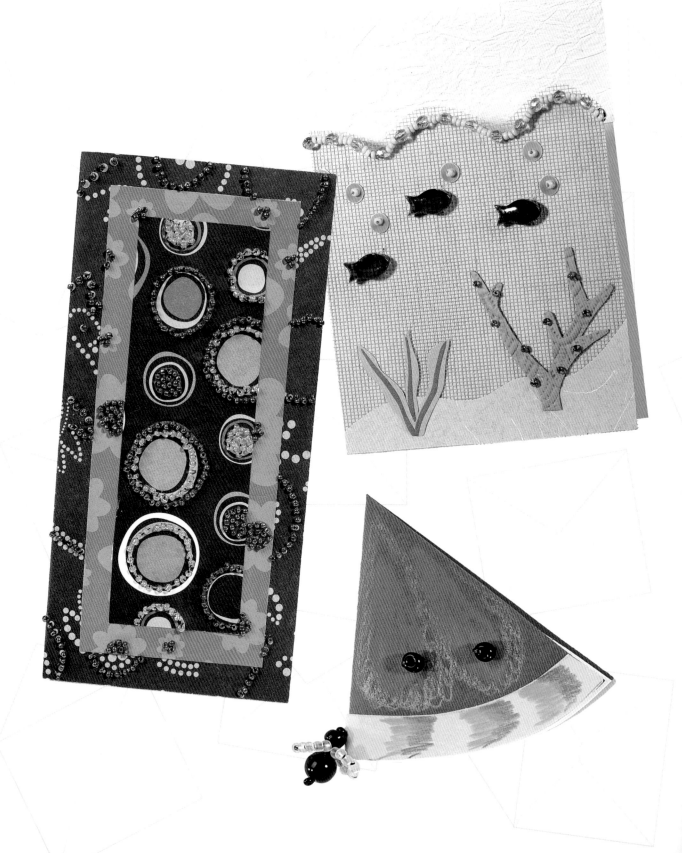

50 Nifty Beaded Cards

Chris Rankin

LARK BOOKS

A Division of Sterling Publishing Co., Inc.
New York / London

SENIOR EDITOR
Ray Hemachandra

EDITOR
Larry Shea

ART DIRECTOR
Kristi Pfeffer

ASSOCIATE ART DIRECTOR
Shannon Yokeley

COVER DESIGNER
Cindy LaBreacht

PHOTOGRAPHER
John Widman

Library of Congress Cataloging-in-Publication Data

Rankin, Chris.
  50 nifty beaded cards / Chris Rankin. -- 1st ed.
      p. cm.
  Includes index.
  ISBN-13: 978-1-60059-146-4 (pb-trade pbk. : alk. paper)
  ISBN-10: 1-60059-146-9 (pb-trade pbk. : alk. paper)
  1. Greeting cards. 2. Beads. I. Title. II. Title: Fifty nifty beaded
cards.
  TT872.R36 2008
  745.594'1--dc22

                                    2007046180

10 9 8 7 6 5 4 3 2 1

First Edition

Published by Lark Books, A Division of
Sterling Publishing Co., Inc.
387 Park Avenue South, New York, NY 10016

© 2008, Lark Books

Distributed in Canada by Sterling Publishing,
c/o Canadian Manda Group, 165 Dufferin Street
Toronto, Ontario, Canada M6K 3H6

Distributed in the United Kingdom by GMC Distribution Services,
Castle Place, 166 High Street, Lewes, East Sussex, England BN7 1XU

Distributed in Australia by Capricorn Link (Australia) Pty Ltd.,
P.O. Box 704, Windsor, NSW 2756 Australia

The written instructions, photographs, designs, patterns, and projects in this volume are intended for the personal use of the reader and may be reproduced for that purpose only. Any other use, especially commercial use, is forbidden under law without written permission of the copyright holder.

Every effort has been made to ensure that all the information in this book is accurate. However, due to differing conditions, tools, and individual skills, the publisher cannot be responsible for any injuries, losses, and other damages that may result from the use of the information in this book.

If you have questions or comments about this book, please contact:
Lark Books
67 Broadway
Asheville, NC 28801
828-253-0467

Manufactured in China

ISBN 13: 978-1-60059-146-4
ISBN 10: 1-60059-146-9

For information about custom editions, special sales, premium and corporate purchases, please contact Sterling Special Sales Department at 800-805-5489 or specialsales@sterlingpub.com.

Contents

Introduction

Anyone can go to the supermarket and plop down some money for a mass-produced card, but the jaws of your nearest and dearest will positively drop when they take these beaded creations from their envelopes. A handmade card means so much more to the recipient; it shows that you invested your time and creativity into making something singularly spectacular that can't be found anywhere else.

Whether you're new to the craft or an experienced card maker, you're sure to find that adding beads to your handmade creations is a great way to make cards that are unique and fun. Take some time to browse a bead store, paying special attention to the smaller beads, as these are mostly what you'll be using in your card projects. Get a feel for which materials, colors, and shapes speak to you, or remind you of a loved one. Even if you've never worked with beads before, the easy techniques in this book will give you a fun introduction into this popular craft.

Read the Basics section that follows to get acquainted with all the materials, tools, and techniques you'll be using. You'll learn about different types of papers, adhesives, and beads, and about the sewing, scrapbooking, and beading tools you may need. You'll also find instructions for making card stock into a card, and for stitching beads on paper.

Some of these projects may look complicated, but all it really takes to make these wonderful cards is paper, a needle and thread or wire, glue, a few simple tools, some beads of your choice, and your imagination. Many of these cards require nothing more than a few simple stitches. Others give you a chance to create collages, add embossing powder, decorate with stamping, or use fabrics in your designs. Let the designs inspire you—if you'd like to experiment or change something, go right ahead! The point of making these cards is to have fun and produce something all your own. You may end up deciding that what you make is just too beautiful to give away!

Beaded Cards Basics

This first part of the book will serve as a handy reference as you work on creating beaded cards. All of the papers, beads, tools, materials, and supplies discussed relate to the projects in this book. If you're just beginning, buy a few simple materials and tools, and add to your stock as you discover where your interests lie. At the end of this section, you'll learn some basic techniques for making the cards that will become the canvas for your beaded masterpieces.

CARDS AND PAPERS

Selecting paper for cards can seem slightly overwhelming because of all the choices you have, but just think of this process as an adventure. Paper is the basis for most cards, and it is used as the substrate, or base, of the card, as well as an embellishment material.

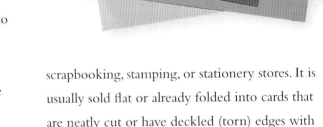

Card Stock

When you're making a basic card, think first about the weight of the paper. If you're going to glue a lot of layers on the front of the card or add embellishments, you'll need a heavier-weight card stock or paper. Just pick up a piece of paper at the store and feel whether it seems substantial enough to hold up other layers of paper, beads, and sequins. You'll probably be folding the paper, so make sure it's thin enough to fold it the way you want. For most cards, a good-quality cover-weight paper or card stock will be fine. Card stock is available in many different colors at craft or art supply,

scrapbooking, stamping, or stationery stores. It is usually sold flat or already folded into cards that are neatly cut or have deckled (torn) edges with accompanying envelopes.

Paper Varieties

With their unique textures and surfaces, hand-made papers make for distinctive cards, but keep in mind they are not as consistent as commercial papers and have no grain. Several projects here use Washi paper, a beautifully patterned hand-made Japanese paper. Decorative scrapbooking papers are another good choice, and they are available in many places—not only craft and art supply stores but also the Internet, your local superstore, and beyond.

If you want to use inks or watercolors for lettering or drawing, it's important to use paper made for those purposes. Acid-free, well-sized paper with a high rag content is the best paper to use. It is made with cotton fibers rather than wood pulp. However, if you're just doodling with colored pens or pencils, you can use any kind of paper.

Be sure to keep the purpose of your card in mind. If you're making a single card that the recipient will want to save, you may want to invest in expensive archival or hand-made papers. However, if you're making disposable cards, you'll want to use less expensive papers.

Many of these projects require found papers, photos, and ephemera. You can find these recycled papers from old magazines, pages from old books, envelopes with interesting postage stamps, postcards, junk mail, manufactured greeting cards, old dress patterns—anything that catches your eye! These materials are the staples of collage artists. The archival quality of these papers often isn't very good, because they are made inexpensively, but they'll do the trick for most cards you create.

Envelopes

The projects in this book do not give instructions on making envelopes, but you can easily buy envelopes for your cards at a stationery store. Again, keep in mind the type of project you're working on: Many of the beaded cards require larger, padded envelopes to accommodate their thicker shape. You can pick envelopes in colors to match your cards or special envelopes made from fabric, hemp, and other materials.

BEADS, BEADS, BEADS!

Now for the fun part—the beads! Beads come in zillions of colors and materials ranging from plastic to bone. The incredible variety available today is an indication of the growing interest in beads. Here's a quick overview of the basic bead information you'll need for the projects in this book.

seed beads

Sizing

Beads are measured in millimeters. For people more accustomed to inches, the comparison chart below should help you as you shop. You can buy beads individually or in strands. Most strands are 16 inches (40.6 cm) long, with the number of beads on each strand determined by individual size. Most of the projects call for smaller beads, and in particular seed beads.

Bead Varieties

Here are the major types of beads you'll encounter:

Seed beads, used often in the following projects, have their own sizing system. It is written as, for example, 6/0, 7/0, 9/0, and so on—the higher the number, the smaller the bead. However, many of these projects do not have a given size for the seed bead listed. Just use your own judgment and pick a color and a size that appeals to you.

10

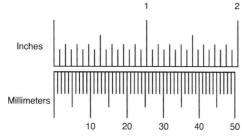

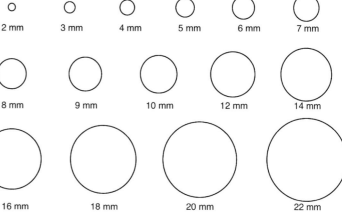

2 mm	3 mm	4 mm	5 mm	6 mm	7 mm
8 mm	9 mm	10 mm	12 mm	14 mm	
16 mm	18 mm	20 mm	22 mm		

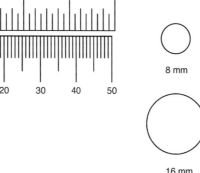
crystal beads

Bugle beads are thin, hollow tubes of glass.

Bone beads can be made from the bones of yaks, camels, cattle, or goats.

Crystal beads are made from leaded glass. They can be clear or colored and are easily faceted, which gives them a lovely, light-reflective quality.

Glass beads come in endless varieties as well, but be careful using glass in these projects. You would not want your beads to break in the mail!

Metal beads can be made from base metal, silver, gold, aluminum, steel, copper, lead-free pewter, or brass. You can also use foreign coins as metal beads in your projects.

Resin and **plastic beads** offer a contemporary option. They often sport translucent surfaces in appealing, bright colors.

Crimp beads aren't traditional beads—they are used in jewelry making to secure the ends of beading wire to hold beads in place. Use them on your cards to space beads at intervals along a wire.

bicone

briolette

rondelle

wheel

drop

Bead Shapes

Bead shapes are, for the most part, descriptive. You can probably figure out what a "rectangle" or "square" bead looks like. Below are some common, not-so-obvious descriptions of beads you may use in the following projects:

- **Bicone**—two cones fused end to end
- **Briolette**—pear-shaped with triangular facets
- **Button**—any shape slightly puffed or domed
- **Disk**—a slice of a cylinder
- **Drop**—a fattened teardrop
- **Faceted**—any shape where curved lines have been squared off into facets
- **Filigree**—a hollow bead with a decorative network of surface lines
- **Nugget**—organically shaped lump
- **Rondelle**—flat and circular
- **Wheel**—a basic wheel shape with diamond-faceted, outward-facing sides

TOOLS

A tool kit for making cards includes scissors, a craft knife, a cutting mat, and a ruler. This section covers those basics and other tools that you may need.

Craft Knife

You'll find yourself reaching for your craft knife often when making cards. This tool works well for making very accurate small cuts, such as windows and small shapes. Always keep a set of fresh blades on hand, since a dull blade will drag and leave a ragged edge. Choose a version that's easy to grip, and hold the knife at a 45° angle to create crisp cuts.

Ruler, Square, and Triangle

To guide the craft knife, use a metal ruler or other ruling device. A steel square is also great to have on hand, especially if you're squaring and cutting larger sheets of paper. Triangles come in handy for scoring and cutting paper shapes.

Cutting Mat or Glass

Always place a self-healing cutting mat beneath the paper you're cutting with a craft knife. The mat will protect the blades of the knife while keeping the papers from curling. Because it's marked with a measuring grid, the mat can also be used like a ruler. As an alternative, you can cut paper on a sheet of glass, which some card makers prefer. Tape the edges of the glass to protect your fingers.

Scissors

You'll find that you frequently use scissors to cut sheets of paper and small decorative items. Keep both a long-bladed and short-bladed pair on hand for different needs. The blades should always be sharp and clean, just like the blades of your craft knife.

You'll also find many uses for decorative-edged scissors that cut a variety of different edges. You can use them simply because you like the look they create, or to emulate the edges of things such as old photos, postage stamps, or fabric rickrack.

Bone Folder

This bookbinding tool is essential for scoring paper and smoothing out creases if you're making folded cards. Bone folders are made from actual bone, resin, or wood. They come in several sizes.

Brayer

Resembling a paint roller, this tool is typically used to spread ink for printing. When making cards, you can use it to flatten papers and to evenly press down materials and images you are attaching on top of your card.

Paper Cutter

If you have access to a paper cutter with a large swinging arm, it's perfect for dividing up larger sheets of paper to make cards. And buying larger sheets can save you money if you're making a lot of cards.

Tapes

You can use clear double-sided tape to adhere decorative pieces to cards. Foam tape is great for creating a three-dimensional effect, since it lifts the element off the card. Plain cellophane tape is great for securing ends of thread.

Hole and Shaped Punches

The traditional round hole punch from an office supply store comes in handy for punching small holes in sheets of paper, and you can also find square punches and circle cutters in different sizes. Besides these geometric punches, you'll find an array of shaped punches of various sizes in the scrapbooking and paper sections of craft supply stores.

Stamps

You can purchase rubber stamps in a wide variety of sizes at a craft supply store, a stamp store, or on the Web, or you can cut your own from rubber. For decorating a series of cards, stamps are handy because you can easily replicate the image.

Heat Gun

This small blower heats air to a temperature that's safe for paper projects. You can use it to dry glues more quickly or emboss inks with embossing powders.

Eyelet Setting Tool

Eyelets function somewhat like grommets but are made up of a single piece instead of two pieces. Use the accompanying setting tool to roll down the backside of the eyelet to hold it in place.

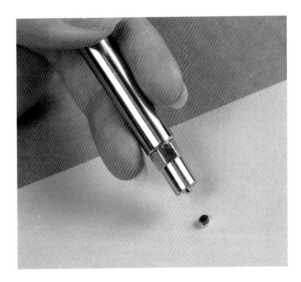

Sewing Tools

You can hand- or machine-stitch paper cards to produce beautiful results. Most of these projects require hand-stitching beads onto paper, but you'll use a sewing machine on a few for other embellishments. For stitching by hand, you'll need a sharp embroidery or tapestry needle for punching the holes before you insert the thread with a smaller needle. Doing this first clean punch in the paper will prevent tears and rough edges. You may also want to use a beading needle for stringing beads. These come in different sizes; the larger the number, the bigger the needle.

Use a sewing machine to decorate your card with random stitching as a background effect, embroider complex designs or names on the front of a card, or attach thicker pieces of paper or cloth to a card.

Beading Tools

For many of the following projects, you'll need pliers and wire cutters to work with wire.

Chain-nose pliers have tapered jaws that are rounded on the outside, flat on the inside. **Needle-nose pliers** are similar to chain-nose pliers, but have even longer tapered jaws. You can use them when making wrapped loops or for shaping wire. **Round-nose pliers**, with their tapered, round jaws, shape wire and are essential for making simple and wrapped loops used for attaching beads. **Wire cutters** need to cut flush to avoid pesky bits of wire poking into your card.

SUPPLIES AND MATERIALS

Once you have your tool kit—basic or more advanced—put together, here are some of the materials you'll need to make cards.

Adhesives

There are many choices for adhering paper or other decorative elements to your cards. Begin by buying a common white craft glue (PVA, or polyvinyl acetate) for general purposes. It's permanent, holds well, and dries clear. For tiny pieces, try out a glue pen, which allows you to trace a small amount of glue onto a specific area. For heavy-duty jobs, you may want to use fast-bonding cyanoacrylate glue, or a heated glue gun.

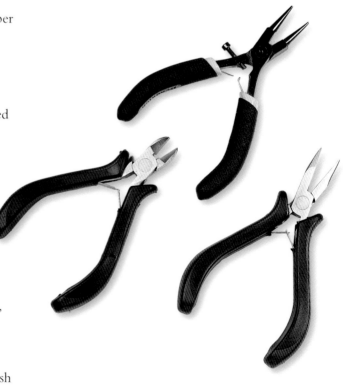

Pens, Pencils, and Markers

Writing and drawing supplies will naturally find their way into your card-making arsenal. It's great to have sharp graphite pencils for marking and colored pencils, pens, and markers that you can grab for adding lettering, simple drawings, or color.

Stamping Inks

There are lots of stamping inks available, but for most purposes, you can use regular dye-based inks (standard "office" inks) or pigment inks. Dye-based inks work best on coated paper. Pigment inks are thicker inks that are opaque and slow to dry, but more resistant to fading than dye-based inks. They work well on absorbent, uncoated paper, such as card stock, and are the ink of choice for embossing.

Embossing Powders

To create raised stamped surfaces, there are many embossing powders in various colors. These fine powders come in small jars. After you sprinkle the powder onto wet pigment inks, shake off the excess powder onto a piece of paper and return it to the jar. Then, use your heat gun to melt the powder and create a beautiful raised design.

Threads

For sewing beads on cards, you'll need a spool or card of beading thread, the most common of which is a single nylon strand. These threads come in slightly different diameters or weights, so choose one that works well with your beads. For hand-stitching on cards, embroidery floss or waxed linen is a good choice. If you plan to machine-stitch cards, keep a stash of threads on hand to give yourself lots of choices. Rayon, cotton, and polyester thread all work equally well with paper.

Wire

Very thin, sturdy beading wire is used to attach beads in some of the projects. Look for a size that is strong, but won't weigh down your paper. Many projects use 26-gauge wire. An alternative to wire is a head pin, which is a short length of wire with one flattened or decorative end that acts as a stop for beads.

Found Objects and Natural Materials

Look around the house and yard and you'll find tons of "stuff" you can use to decorate cards. Found objects such as metal washers, buttons, or foreign coins can add visual interest to your design. Natural materials such as butterfly wings, feathers, pressed flowers, and leaves make lovely additions, too.

Scrapbooking Materials

Head to the scrapbooking aisle of your local craft store to find items that will give your cards instant pizzazz. Besides paper, you'll find miniatures, stickers, dots, letters, and more embellishments for any occasion.

TECHNIQUES

In this section, we'll cover the most basic techniques you'll need to turn a blank piece of paper into an attractive beaded card.

Cutting, Scoring, and Folding a Blank Card

You may find an amazing paper you want to make into a blank card, or you simply may want to save money by cutting and folding your own cards. Making your own cards is easy with some basic equipment and patience.

1 When you decide on the size of card that you want, use a paper trimmer or a craft knife and a cutting mat to neatly trim a piece of card stock or other paper to twice the size of one card panel. For instance, if you want to make a 4 x 5-inch (10.2 x 12.7 cm) card, cut a piece of paper that is 8 x 5 inches (20.4 x 12.7 cm).

2 On the side of the paper that falls inside your card, mark a line with a light pencil mark along the fold line. Place your ruler along this line and score the line with the pointed end of a bone folder (see photo below). Doing this breaks the top fibers in the paper so the paper will fold crisply.

3 Fold the card along the line you scored. Beginning at the top of the card, press the edge of the card with the curved portion of the bone folder to make a neat fold, and you're ready to go!

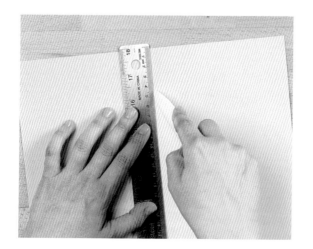

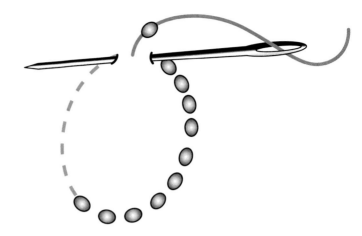

Stitching and Beading Your Card

Attach single sequins, charms, beads, and buttons to your cards the same way you'd attach them to fabric—by starting at the back, threading through the hole or holes, going through to the back again, and then knotting in the back. Then just add a dab of glue to keep the knot from coming undone. It's a good idea to pre-punch the holes you'll be sewing through to avoid a ragged look.

If you're adding more than one bead, button, or sequin, you may want to use a beading needle and the method shown above: Sew each bead on separately, threading it onto the needle, poking the needle back through the paper, and securing it with a backstitch before moving on to the next add-in. A thin needle, strong thread, and beads with a small opening are great for paper projects. Instead of thread, you may choose to use monofilament or wire. Add a dab of strong glue in the back to secure the final knot in place.

The Projects

Now it's time for the really fun and creative part of the book—dozens of truly nifty cards you can make yourself. All of these cards are simple to make, though some do require you to use particular techniques, such as stitching, embossing, or setting eyelets. Browse a while through this gallery of eye-catching cards, noting which tools and materials different cards require, before deciding which will be your first handmade creation. And remember: The designs here are intended to be sparks that light your imagination. You can always substitute your own choice of colors and materials to make something even more special and one-of-a-kind.

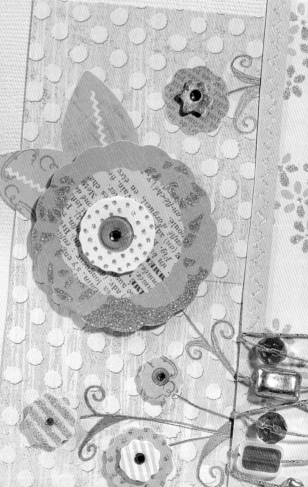

Kim Grant

Spring Maiden

Celebrate a new season with bouquets of beaded blossoms.

Designer: **JANE REEVES**

MATERIALS & TOOLS

- Card stock, 8½ x 11 inches (21.6 x 27.9 cm)
- Bone folder
- Speckled white paper, 7½ x 10¼ inches (19 x 26 cm)
- Rubber stamp and ink pad
- Fabric square, off-white
- Floral fabric cut outs and scraps
- Floral background fabric, 5 x 7¾ inches (12.7 x 19.7 cm)
- Sewing needle
- White thread
- Seed beads
- Glue stick
- Awl
- Ribbon

STEP BY STEP

1 Fold the card stock and craft paper in half and smooth with the bone folder. Place the craft paper inside the card stock.

2 Stamp the image on the fabric square and arrange the fabric flowers, scraps, and stamped square onto the background fabric.

3 Sew the arrangement into place and sew beads on the fabric flowers and around the stamped square.

4 Glue the arrangement on the front of the card stock.

5 Using the awl, punch three equally spaced holes along the fold line of the card stock and craft paper.

6 Lace one end of the ribbon through the middle hole on the card stock and loop it through the top hole, down to the bottom hole, and back through the middle. Tie the two ends of the ribbon in a bow on the outside of the card.

Easy Early Bird

These cards are wonderful in their simplicity, requiring only elementary drawing skills and a wide-open imagination. The gray and brown beads add a rustic touch.

Designer: **JEAN TOMASO MOORE**

MATERIALS & TOOLS

- Bone folder
- Card stock
- Scissors
- Decorative scissors (optional)
- Various decorative papers
- Double-sided tape
- Ruler
- Pencil
- Small brush for glue
- Craft glue
- Gray and brown flat-sided 5 mm beads

■ STEP BY STEP

1 Fold the card stock and smooth it with the bone folder. Cut the background papers. The bird design uses gray decorative paper cut with pinking shears layered over red decorative paper. Apply it to the card stock using double-sided tape.

2 Sketch a simple design onto the top layer of your card, such as a bird, heart, or other basic shape.

3 Use the small brush to apply glue along the pencil line. Attach the flat-sided beads onto the glue. Work in small sections so the glue does not dry out. Continue applying the glue and beads until you complete the design.

These beads are neutral and super versatile. Use them to outline basic shapes, like squares or hearts.

Mesmerizing Mermaid

This lucky mermaid flaunts a gorgeous Japanese Washi paper tail. Experiment with funky fibers for her seaworthy hair.

Designer: **LISA GLICKSMAN**

MATERIALS & TOOLS

- 2 sheets light green or blue card stock, 5 x 7 inches (12.7 x 17.8 cm)
- Decorative cool-toned paper, 4½ x 6½ inches (11.4 x 16.5 cm)
- Craft glue
- Pencil
- Scissors
- Washi paper
- Toothpick
- Beads
- Tweezers (for easy version)
- Beading needle and thread (for more difficult version)
- Fibers

STEP BY STEP

1 Glue the decorative background paper to the card stock.

2 Draw a mermaid outline on the blue or green card stock, then cut it out. If you can't draw well, find a mermaid illustration online, print it out, and use it to trace the shape of the mermaid.

3 Use the mermaid shape to outline and cut out the Washi paper fish tail, making sure to cut the tail slightly larger around the edges than the mermaid shape. Adhere the Washi paper tail to the mermaid body.

4 For the quick and easy version of this card, apply strong glue with a toothpick to the backs of the beads. Choose flatter and lighter beads if you are going to use this method. Tweezers might be helpful for bead placement. Glue the beads onto the face, body, and tail.

5 For the more difficult (but more secure) version, sew the beads on the mermaid. First prick through the paper mermaid for bead placement, then sew on the beads. For exact placement of the beads, reinforce the beads to the paper by applying tiny dots of glue with a toothpick. Use this method if you want to use heavier or rounded beads.

6 Attach fibers to the mermaid's head with glue.

7 Mount the mermaid on the card. Put touches of glue underneath various parts of the hair to secure it to the card.

25

Collage Crazy

*This card is dripping with personality—
add drawings, photographs, stamps, fabric,
comics, and papers to make it all your own.*

Designer: **CANDIE COOPER**

MATERIALS & TOOLS

- Small scraps of paper, photos, stamps, and fabric
- Glue stick
- Handmade card blank, 6¼ x 4½ inches (15.9 x 11.4 cm)
- Fabric glue
- Seed or bugle beads
- Needle and thread
- 20 inches (50.8 cm) of novelty fibers, recycled silk and ribbon
- Glass beads

■ STEP BY STEP

1 Assemble approximately nine mini-collages each measuring approximately 1 inch (2.5 cm) square and comprised of papers and fabric. Glue the layers as you go.

2 You can stitch beads onto pieces of fabric or to the card by running the needle and thread up from the back side of the fabric or card, stringing a bead onto the needle and putting the needle back through the material. Repeat to add another bead or tie the thread off and trim away the tails.

3 Glue each of the mini-collages to the front side of the card blank using the project photo as a guide.

4 Add simple straight stitches around the collages by hand or with a machine, as seen around the teakettle collage in the upper left corner. You can add extra security to the back side of the card's stitches with a dot of glue.

5 Open the card, lay the novelty fibers down the center and close the card. Bring the ends of the fibers together at the top left corner of the card and tie in a knot so the tails hang down the side. Slide some beads onto the tails of the yarn and knot in place. Trim the tails to desired length.

Swirly Pearly Paisley

Pearl beads make this throwback paisley pattern pop!

Designer: **JOAN K. MORRIS**

THE PROJECTS

MATERIALS & TOOLS

- Purple sewing thread
- Beading needle
- Blue, purple, and gold floral paisley paper, 3¼ x 5 inches (8.3 x 12.7 cm)
- Purple seed beads
- Gold seed beads
- Pearl seed beads
- Pearl beads, ⅜ inch (1 cm)
- Pale purple card stock, 6 x 8 inches (15.2 x 20.3 cm)
- Glue stick

▌ STEP BY STEP

1 Starting from the back side and corner of the paisley paper, stitch beads onto the floral paper so that the bead colors match up with the pattern colors, as shown in the project photo. Place one bead per stitch.

2 Repeat this with all the beads. Tie a knot in the back every five or six beads, in case the thread breaks. Add new thread when needed.

3 Fold the 6 x 8-inch (15.2 x 20.3 cm) card stock in half so you have a 4 x 6-inch (10.2 x 15.2 cm) card with a side fold.

4 Using the glue stick, cover the back of the beaded paper with glue. Run the glue over the threads and the paper.

5 Place the beaded and glued paper in position on the folded card stock. Rub with light pressure to set the glue.

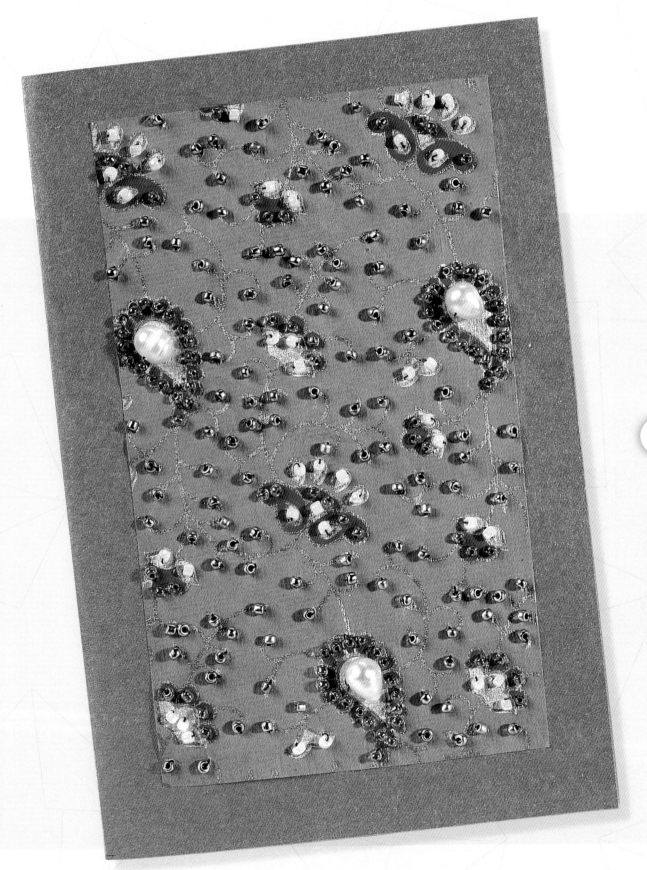

Cupcake in a Cinch

A sweet greeting card sprinkled with candy-colored beads makes any gift a treat.

Designer: **DEBBIE CRANE**

THE PROJECTS

MATERIALS & TOOLS

- Lavender card stock folded to 3 x 4 inches (7.6 x 10.2 cm)
- Colored pencil
- Black marker
- Two pieces decorative paper in coordinating colors, 2 x 3 inches (5.1 x 7.6 cm)
- Scissors
- Glue stick
- Craft glue
- 15 beads for sprinkles, 2 mm
- Red scrap paper

■ STEP BY STEP

1 Draw a loose border around the front of the card with the colored pencil, then draw a looser line inside the pencil border with the black marker.

2 Draw a cupcake and frosting shape onto decorative papers and cut out. Assemble and glue the cupcake onto the front of the card with the glue stick.

3 Dot craft glue onto the "frosting" and add the bead sprinkles. Cut a small circle from red scrap paper for the cherry and glue on top of the frosting.

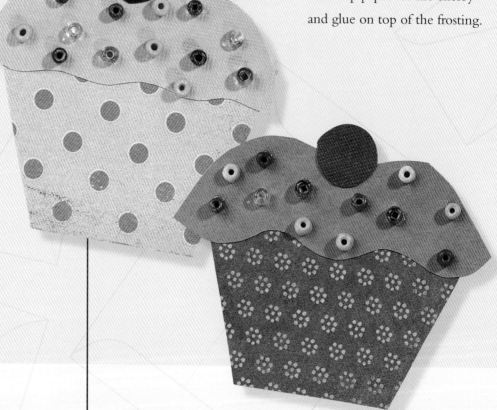

Swingin' Chandelier

Turn on the glamour with this opulent chandelier. No drawing needed—just find some clip art or an illustration online!

Designer: **JOAN K. MORRIS**

MATERIALS & TOOLS

- Mustard color card stock, 4 x 6 inches (10.2 x 15.2 cm)
- Clip art chandelier design
- Copy machine
- 22 oval pearl beads
- 21 round crystal beads
- 18 oval crystal beads
- Black sewing thread
- Beading needle
- Light brown card stock, 8 x 10 inches (20.3 x 25.4 cm)
- Glue stick

■ STEP BY STEP

1 Copy or print the clip art chandelier onto the mustard-colored card stock.

2 Using the project photo as a guide, stitch the oval pearl beads onto the chandelier, starting from the back side of the card. The oval pearl beads replace the candles.

3 Place a round crystal bead and an oval crystal bead onto the thread, making sure the beads are hanging as if from a chandelier. Run the needle and thread to the back of the card and tie a knot with the thread.

4 Keeping the thread attached, run the needle and thread up from the back of the card where you want to place the next crystal. Repeat running the thread back down and tying the knot.

5 Repeat step 4 for the rest of the crystals and for the candles.

6 Fold the 8 x 10-inch (20.3 x 25.4 cm) card stock in half, creating a 5 x 8-inch (12.7 x 20.3 cm) card with a side fold.

7 Using the glue stick, glue the beaded piece in position on the folded card stock. Rub lightly to set the glue.

Merci, Chérie

Black lace, floral paper, and dangling beads lend a decidedly French feel to this thank-you tag.

Designer: **CARLA SCHAUER**

MATERIALS & TOOLS

- Scissors
- Black word-printed paper
- Yellow floral print paper
- Red floral print paper
- Glue stick
- Small needle
- 7 black 4 x 8 mm bicone beads
- 7 red 3 mm glass beads
- 7 light yellow 4 x 6 mm glass faceted beads
- 7 head pins, 2 inches (5.1 cm) each
- Wire cutters
- 5 inches (12.7 cm) of black lace
- Craft glue
- Aqua paper daisy, 2 inches (5.1 cm) in diameter
- Black flower rub-on designs
- Black script sticker letters
- Red chalk and applicator

■ STEP BY STEP

1 Cut the black printed paper to 2½ x 4 inches (6.4 x 10.2 cm), and trim one end into tag shape.

2 Cut the yellow floral paper to 2 inches (5.1 cm) wide, and the red floral paper to 1 inch (2.5 cm) wide. Trim the short sides of each piece in identical tag shape, and adhere horizontally to the black tag, allowing 1/16 inch (0.2 cm) of black to show around the edge. Using a needle, punch seven small holes, equal distance apart, at the intersection of red and yellow paper.

3 Thread one red, black, and yellow bead onto each of the head pins. Attach head pins through the pre-punched holes, and bend the back of the pins flat with back side of tag. Trim the excess pin length.

4 Attach lace to tag using white craft glue, covering paper intersection and head pin tops. Wrap ends around tag and secure with glue on back.

5 Glue the flower to the right side of tag, and rub the flower design in the center.

6 Adhere sticker phrase "Merci" to top left of tag, and apply red chalk gently over top of phrase to add definition. The tag can be mounted on card stock trimmed to size, in order to neaten the back of tag and cover the ends of the head pins and lace.

THE PROJECTS

Boogie Woogie Bugle Beads

Bugle beads are easy to use and adapt well to linear patterns.
Build a whole house in less than an hour!

Designer: **JEAN TOMASO MOORE**

MATERIALS & TOOLS

- Card stock
- Bone folder
- Pencil
- Ruler
- Various decorative papers or tape
- Beading needle
- Bugle beads
- 32-gauge beading wire
- Cellophane tape
- Wire cutters
- Small accent beads
- Small flower stickers
- Carpet tape

■ STEP BY STEP

1 Fold the card stock and smooth with the bone folder. Lightly sketch a house design onto the card stock with a pencil.

2 Cut out a piece of decorative paper or tape for the "ground." Adhere to the bottom edge of the card.

3 Use the needle to poke a hole into the card stock at strategic points so that you can begin and end each segment of your design; for example, poke holes for the top and bottom of the sides or roof of the house.

4 Thread bugle beads onto the wire. Poke one end of the wire back to front through the pinhole at the start point of your design and use cellophane tape to hold the tail of the wire in place on the inside of the card. Pull the beaded wire to the next pinhole, cutting the wire to finish that segment of the design (leave enough wire to push back through and tape to the inside of the card).

For a fun variation on this card, put flower stickers inside a bugle-beaded grid.

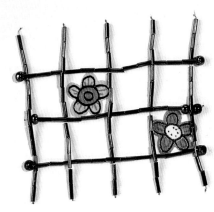

5 Continue to construct the lines of your design in the same manner, working each segment separately and leaving the wire tails secured with tape on the inside of the card. Use accent beads to embellish the design if desired and add flower stickers for extra color and texture.

6 Cut a piece of card stock to fit inside the card. Use carpet tape to adhere the card stock inside the card to cover the exposed wire.

True Love

Send wishes of love with alphabet beads dancing across a patterned heart.

Designer: **BRANDY LOGAN**

MATERIALS & TOOLS

- Pink card stock, 5 x 8½ inches (12.7 x 21.6 cm)
- Bone folder
- Craft glue
- Stripe patterned paper, 1 x 5 inches (2.5 x 12.7 cm)
- Black pen
- Heart cutout from patterned paper
- Heart chipboard sticker
- 26-gauge wire
- 6 red glass beads
- 2 heart beads
- Alphabet beads to spell "Amore," or your choice of message
- Pliers (any type)

■ STEP BY STEP

1 Fold the card stock in half and smooth with the bone folder.

2 Glue the striped paper across the bottom edge of the card stock.

3 Draw a dotted line across the top edge of the striped paper strip.

4 Glue the heart cutout above the dotted line.

5 Adhere the chipboard heart sticker to the center of the heart cutout.

6 Take a piece of wire and attach beads to spell out your message. Add red beads as accents on both ends. Curl the wire ends using pliers.

7 Adhere the beaded wire across the bottom of the heart with the craft glue.

Flower Song

This vintage-inspired design has delicate embellishments to charm and delight.

Designer: **SHARON ROHLOFF**

MATERIALS & TOOLS

- Sage green card stock, 8½ x 11 inches (21.6 x 27.9 cm)
- Decorative scissors
- Creamy polka dot paper, 3½ x 4¼ inches (8.9 x 10.8 cm)
- Gold pen
- Green/cream alphabet paper, 5 x 3¾ inches (12.7 x 9.5 cm)
- Double-sided tape
- Scissors
- Clip art vintage bird image
- Needle and thread
- 5 small pearls
- Gold glitter glue
- Handwriting background stamp
- Gold ink
- Sewing machine (optional)
- 2 bronze eyelets
- Eyelet setting tool
- Pink ribbon, 9½ inches (24.1 cm)

THE PROJECTS

■ STEP BY STEP

1 Fold the green card stock in half. Use decorative scissors to cut the polka dot paper to 3½ x 4¼ inches (8.9 x 10.8 cm) and gild its edges with the gold pen. Adhere to green alphabet paper, ¼ inch (0.6 cm) down from the top edge, using double-sided tape.

2 Cut out vintage bird image, including border. Affix bird image on top of polka dot paper, ¼ inch (0.6 cm) down from the top edge, using double-sided tape.

3 Punch holes through the five largest roses with a needle (through all three paper layers) and sew pearls onto the image. Lightly dot some of the image's leaves with gold glitter glue and allow them to dry.

4 Apply the handwriting background stamp to the lower right hand corner of the bird image in gold ink, overlapping the underlying papers.

5 Center and adhere the layered papers to the green cardstock with double-sided tape. If desired, machine-sew all papers together through the border of the bird image.

6 Inset two eyelets below the bird image, 1½ inches (3.8 cm) from each side of the card, and 1¼ inches (3.2 cm) up from the card base. Thread in the ribbon and tie in a bow.

A Bead with a View

*Bead lovers will adore you when you
give them a card they can disassemble
and use for their own bead-acious reasons.*

Designer: **TERRY TAYLOR**

MATERIALS & TOOLS

- Foam core board
- Craft knife and sharp blades
- Ruler
- Decorative papers
- Spray adhesive
- 18-gauge wire, approximately
  4 inches (10.2 cm) long
- Focal bead
- Needle-nose pliers
- Wire cutters

STEP BY STEP

1 Cut a piece of foam core board
to the size desired for your card.
The cards pictured here are 5 x 4
inches (12.7 x 10.2 cm). Always
cut foam core board with a new
blade. Change your blade often;
dulled blades create ugly edges.

2 Measure the dimensions of
your focal bead to determine
the size window you will need
to showcase it. The windows on

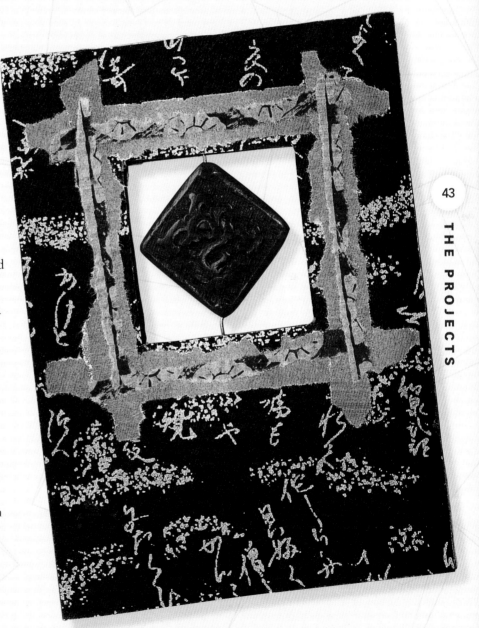

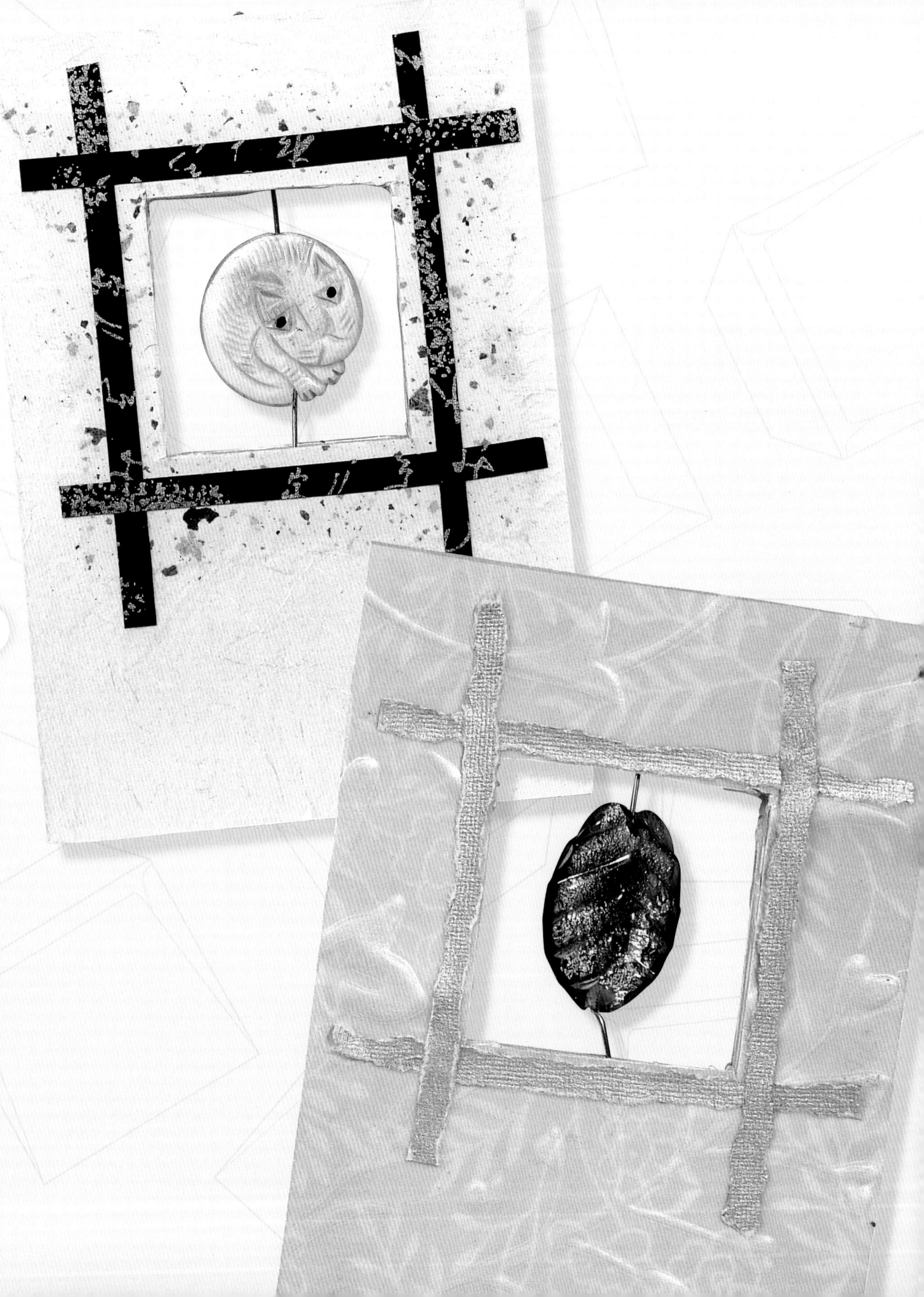

the cards pictured are approximately 1½ inches (3.8 cm) square. Mark the window on the foam core board. Cut it out with the craft knife.

3 Adhere decorative paper to one side of the foam core board. Trim the excess paper and cut out the window shape. Adhere a second piece of paper to the opposite side, trim it, and cut out the window shape.

4 Straighten the wire by pulling it between your fingers. Center the wire at the top of the card. Push the wire down into the edge of the foam core board until it emerges from the opposite side into the window.

Thread your focal bead onto the wire, then continue to push the wire to the opposite edge of the board.

5 Place your pliers directly below the bead, grasp the wire, and give the pliers a twist to make a gentle kink in the wire. Enlarge the kink as needed to hold the bead in place.

6 Grasp the top of the wire at the top of the card and lift it up a bit. Trim the wire with the cutters and make a 90° bend in the wire. Push the wire back down. The bend will suspend the bead in the window.

Chinese Beadwork

The Chinese character on this card is the symbol for good health. Cutting a window out of the card will let light shine through the beads.

Designer: **RAIN NEWCOMB**

MATERIALS & TOOLS

- 2 pieces of card stock, 5½ x 8 inches (14 x 20.3 cm)
- Bone folder
- Pencil
- Piece of loom work*
- Cardboard
- Craft knife
- Masking tape
- Glue stick
- Cyanoacrylate glue (optional)

* If you don't know how to do loom work, buy an unfinished piece at a crafts or bead store.

■ STEP BY STEP

1 Fold both pieces of card stock in half and smooth with the bone folder. Trace the outline of the loom work on the inside front of one piece of card stock using a pencil.

2 Set the card stock on a piece of cardboard and use the craft knife to cut out the outline. Cut slightly inside the lines. (If you're using a piece of finished loom work, cut the shape ⅛ inch [0.3 cm] smaller than the outline.)

3 Repeat steps 1 and 2, cutting a hole in the second piece of card stock.

4 Sandwich the loom work between both pieces of card stock, centering it in the hole you cut out. You can tape down any threads from the loom work with masking tape.

5 Glue both pieces of card stock together with the glue stick. Make sure that no threads are showing on the outside of the card.

6 If you're using a finished piece of loom work, you won't be able to sandwich it between two pieces of card stock. Instead, use the cyanoacrylate glue to secure the beads on the outer ⅛ inch (0.3 mm) of the loom work to the card stock.

THE PROJECTS

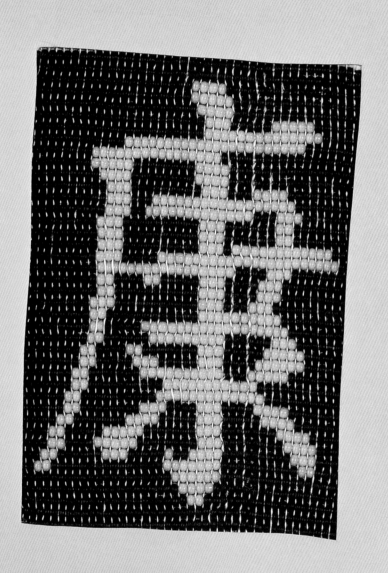

Polka Dotted Flower Power

This graphic ensemble is black and white and cute all over.

Designer: **CANDIE COOPER**

MATERIALS & TOOLS

- Scissors
- 1 sheet black craft felt, 3 inches (7.6 cm) square
- Red leather flower trim, 1⅛ inch (2.6 cm) wide
- Sewing needle
- Black thread
- 3 silver faceted 4 mm beads
- Glue stick
- White card stock strip, 2¾ x 8 inches (7 x 20.3 cm)
- Black card blank, 4½ x 6¼ inches (11.4 x 15.9 cm)
- 2 pieces of black ribbon with white polka dots, 8 x ⅝ inches (20.3 x 1.6 cm)
- Craft glue
- 2 pieces of black and white striped ribbon, 8 x ⅜ inches (20.3 x 1 cm)
- 12 red 1/0 seed beads
- 2 pieces of white ribbon with black polka dots, 4 x ¼ inches (10.2 x 0.6 cm)
- 2 clear 12 mm leaf beads
- White thread
- 2 black seed beads

■ STEP BY STEP

1 Cut three small black felt circles ¼ to ⅜ inch (0.6 to 1 cm) in diameter.

2 Cut three flowers from the trim. Thread the needle with black thread. Place the felt circle on the flower and poke the needle from the back of the flower through to the felt. String one silver bead and put the needle back through the felt and flower and tie off. Repeat two more times.

3 Glue the white card stock strip down the middle section of the card, folding over the excess and adhering with the glue stick.

4 Glue a piece of black with white polka dot ribbon down the far edge of the card and fold the ends over to the inside of the card and glue. Glue the striped ribbon next to the polka dot ribbon, folding over and gluing the excess.

5 Stitch red beads to some of the white polka dots on the ribbon by bringing the needle from the back to the front, stringing one red seed bead and putting the needle back through the same hole and out at the polka dot. When you are finished, tie the thread off and add a dot of craft glue to secure.

6 Using the project photo as a guide, lay the white ribbon, flowers, and clear leaves in the center of the card. Thread the sewing needle with white thread as before. For each ribbon, bring the needle through the back of the ribbon, leaf bead, and black seed bead. Then put the needle down through the leaf, bead, and ribbon. Repeat and tie off the thread.

7 Glue the top of the white ribbons into place followed by the flower embellishments. You can cut and glue a smaller piece of white card stock inside the card to hide the folded-over ribbon and paper ends.

Homage to Mondrian

This card is inspired by Piet Mondrian, the Dutch painter who created bold compositions featuring balanced rectangles of white and primary colors surrounded by strong black lines.

Designer: **ELIZABETH BECK**

MATERIALS & TOOLS

- Ruler
- Pencil
- Watercolor paper
- Black permanent marker
- Red, yellow, and blue acrylic paints
- Flat paintbrush
- Scissors
- Yellow card stock
- Glass beads chosen to match paint colors, irregularly shaped
- 18-gauge floral stem wire
- Wire cutters
- Pliers (any type)
- Cyanoacrylate glue

■ STEP BY STEP

1 Use a ruler, a pencil, and a light touch to design a square on watercolor paper with multiple intersecting lines inside of it. Using the ruler again, go over the pencil lines with a thick black marker.

2 With a flat paintbrush, paint some of the rectangles red, yellow, and blue. Intersperse each color through the painting to create balance, and leave several rectangles white.

3 Carefully cut out your artwork at the edge of your square. Mount your Mondrian-inspired painting on yellow card stock, near the top, leaving room for beading.

4 Place a red, a yellow, and a blue bead on 18-gauge floral stem wire. Cut your wire to size and curve the ends of the wire into curlicues with pliers, in contrast to the straight edges of the painting.

5 Use small spots of cyanoacrylate glue on each bead to attach the beaded wire to the yellow card stock.

6 For a variation, experiment with different color palettes: Shades of pinks and greens; turquoise, red, and brown; or monochromatic hues might better suit your mood!

La Sirena

This mermaid gift tag makes use of quilting fabric enhanced by beading. The siren design is taken from La Loteria, *a Mexican card game of chance.*

Designer: **SUSAN McBRIDE**

MATERIALS & TOOLS

- Small piece of quilting fabric with "La Sirena" or other similar image
- Scissors
- Seed beads: blue, green, and clear glass
- 1 freshwater pearl
- Needle
- Thread
- Craft knife
- Straightedge
- Cutting mat
- Textured paper
- Colorful card stock
- Hot glue gun and glue sticks
- Hole punch
- Raffia

THE PROJECTS

■ STEP BY STEP

1 Carefully cut out the image from the quilting cloth. Thread a needle and sew the seed beads on to the image. The designer for this project sewed amber beads onto the tail of the mermaid and gave the water a little sparkle with clear, blue and green seed beads. The mermaid is holding up a shell, which has a freshwater pearl sewn to it, and finally an amber bead was added to her hair.

2 With a straightedge on a cutting mat, cut out the textured paper and card stock. This tag was arranged so the layers of paper act as a visual frame for the image of the mermaid. The card stock should be the largest piece, the textured paper next largest, and the fabric the smallest.

3 Glue three pieces together, one on top of the other, using hot glue. Use only a small amount of hot glue on the fabric—too much may bleed through and warp the image.

4 Once the layers of paper and fabric have dried, use a circular paper punch to punch a hole on the top. Thread the hole with raffia and attach it to a gift bag.

5 *La Loteria* has many different types of images, so you can pick the one that suits your gift best: Choose from birds, stars, food, plants, and many more.

Color Fusion

Create mini-sized pieces of artwork by layering and infusing acrylic paints and metallic elements.

Designer: **KIM GRANT**

THE PROJECTS

MATERIALS & TOOLS

- Sheet of 140 lb. watercolor paper, 22 x 30 inches (55.9 x 76.2 cm)
- Acrylic paint, black and various colors
- Flat paintbrush, 2 inches (5.1 cm)
- Mark-making tools
- Gold metallic paint
- Golden mica flake glue
- Palette knife
- Glitter glue
- Ruler
- Pencil
- Paper cutter (optional)
- Scissors
- Hot glue and gun
- Black card stock and envelope, 10 x 6½ inch (25.4 x 16.5 cm)
- Bone folder
- Beads of your choice
- Needle and thread
- Craft glue

■ STEP BY STEP

1 Layer various colors of acrylic paints onto the watercolor paper and let them dry. You will be painting the whole sheet of watercolor paper and cutting it up at the end of the painting process, so do not work small at first.

2 With your mark-making tools and black paint, lay down random black marks. Do not think about where you should put down color, work freely. Create more marks using gold metallic acrylic paint.

3 Spread the mica flakes randomly onto the paper using a palette knife and let them dry. Spread glitter glue randomly onto the paper, also letting it dry.

4 With a paper cutter or scissors, cut the decorated paper

to 4¼ x 5¾ inches (10.8 x 14.6 cm). Glue this to the card stock with a hot glue gun. Once glue dries, fold and smooth the card stock with the bone folder. Attach the beads to the front with stitching or craft glue.

5 Embellish your envelope with leftover snippets of painted watercolor paper and attach them with the hot glue gun.

6 Sign your card! It is a work of art.

Victorian Visions

These aristocratic beauties feature beads and feathers tucked into their hats. These are perfect all-occasion cards for those who appreciate fine detail.

Designer: **SUSAN MOSTEK**

THE PROJECTS

MATERIALS & TOOLS

For purple card:
- Purple suede paper
- Green grosgrain ribbon
- Purple card stock folded to 5½ x 6¾ inches (14 x 17.1 cm)
- Extra purple card stock scrap for layering
- Vintage design corner punch

For blue card:
- Dark blue card stock folded to 5½ inches (14 cm) square
- Dark blue scrap

For both:
- Scissors
- Victorian woman stamp
- Cream card stock
- Black dye ink
- Color pencils
- Glue stick
- Feathers
- Industrial glue
- Pearl bridal spray
- Paper cutter (optional)
- Decorative background paper
- Glue stick
- Double-sided tape
- Light yellow paper

■ STEP BY STEP

1 For both cards: Stamp the woman's face onto a piece of cream card stock using the black dye ink. Color her face and hair with pencils. For the purple card, stamp again onto a piece of purple suede paper and cut out only the collar and hat.

2 For the purple card, attach the suede collar and hat to the stamped design, using a glue stick. Make a bow out of grosgrain ribbon and attach it to her hat. Slip a green feather under the hat. Using the industrial glue, attach the bow and feather to the stamped image and add a pearl bridal spray on top of the feather. For the blue card, cut out an oval from dark blue card stock. Attach a feather and pearl spray onto the reverse of the stamped image, using the industrial glue. Attach the entire piece to the blue cut oval.

3 For the purple card, cut a piece of cream card stock to 4¼ x 5⅛ inches (10.8 x 13 cm). Punch all four corners of the card stock with the punch. Slide a 3¾ x 4⅝-inch (9.5 x 11.7 cm) piece of background paper into the corners of the cream card stock.

4 Finish the purple card by layering cream card stock onto a slightly larger piece of purple card stock, then to a 5⅛ x 6½-inch (13 x 16.5 cm) piece of background paper. Finish by layering all onto a slightly larger piece of cream card stock and finally onto the folded purple card using double-sided tape. Finish the blue card by attaching the oval to a 4¾-inch-square (12.1 cm) piece of background paper. Layer to a slightly larger piece of light yellow card stock and finally to the folded blue card.

Fantastic Orbit

This card is made by photocopying an original collage at two different sizes. Preserve a copy and make as many cards as you'd like!

Designer: **SANDRA EVERTSON**

MATERIALS & TOOLS

- Collage materials (photos, magazines, newspaper print, etc.)
- Scissors
- Card stock, standard sheet
- Decorating chalks
- Decoupage medium
- 26-gauge wire
- Wire cutters
- White glue
- Silk floss
- Small and large hole punches
- Decorative papers
- Safety pin
- Thin beading needle
- Peridot 5 mm beads
- Aqua, garnet, and green glass seed beads

■ STEP BY STEP

1 Compose your collage background on the card stock. The designer of this project cut a circle from an old photo of a child and added color to the cheeks with decorating chalk. The clown suit and dunce hat came from

a sheet music booklet, and the butterfly wings from a science book. The dots on the clown suit are made using various-sized circle hole punches.

2 Photocopy your image so you'll have a smooth beading surface. Make one copy at 100 percent and a second copy at 25 percent.

3 Fold a piece of card stock in half and adhere the large collage copy to it with decoupage medium, making sure the fold in the card stock is at the back of your collage. When dry, cut out the card. Adhere the small copy to the card stock, let it dry and cut it out.

4 Make a lasso-type circle about 2½ inches (6.4 cm) from wire. Glue the "stem" of the lasso to the tip of the finger of the large clown using white glue. Glue a piece of silk floss to the back of the small clown, and using paper "dots" punched with circle punch, adhere ends of floss to the wire structure, between two paper dots. Take the floss through the center of the wire, securing it to the back of the small clown with more paper dots. Continue gluing paper dots along the circle, sandwiching the wire in between. Let dry completely.

5 Pre-poke holes in the body of the card with the tip of a safety pin at every place you want to place a bead. Prevent tangling by threading your needle with about 7 inches (17.8 cm) of floss at a time. Starting at the back and bottom of your card, push the needle up through the front, slide on a 5 mm bead, and then slide on a seed bead. Run the needle back through the hole of the first bead and then back through the card. Add dabs of white glue here and there to help secure the beads.

6 Add beads in the same fashion to the small clown.

7 To create a smooth finish on the inside of the card and to hide stitches, cut a template of the shape of your collage from card stock and adhere it to the inside back of card with decoupage medium.

Beady Bugs Picnic

You won't mind sharing your picnic blanket with these adorable little beaded bugs. Choose from a strawberry, flower, or watermelon-shaped card, or design your own bug snack.

Designer: **SHARON BATEMAN**

MATERIALS & TOOLS

- Card stock: colors used here are pink, red, green, and light green
- Bone folder
- Pencil
- Scissors
- Craft glue
- Colored pencils
- Small needle
- Black or invisible thread
- Yellow and black 5 mm to 7 mm beads (for bees)
- Assorted small black and silver beads
- White paper

■ STEP BY STEP

1 Using the project photo as a guide, fold card stock, smooth with the bone folder, and trace the shape of the flower, strawberry, or watermelon onto the card stock. Cut out on the fold so that the shape becomes two sides of the card. Trace the plant's trim onto the green card stock, cut it out, and glue onto the fruit or flower.

2 When the glue dries, shade your chosen plant with colored pencils. You can add darker green shades to the watermelon rind; purple, white, pink, and black to the flower for more vibrant colors; and black, white, and dark green to the strawberry for definition.

3 Glue or stitch your small black "seeds" to the plant shapes where appropriate.

4 You may want to experiment with making bugs out of the beads until you get a shape you like. To make the fly, bring the needle and thread from the inside back fold to the outside. String on three small black beads, then ten silver beads. Bring your needle and thread through the front of the third black bead again, making a loop of the silver beads for

the wing. Repeat for the other wing, and bring thread through the front of the third black bead again. This time, add a slightly large black bead for the fly's body, and then a small black bead at the end, bringing the needle and thread back through the center of the large black bead and three small black beads and back through the original hole in the card's fold. Tie off the thread.

5 Cut out white paper just a bit smaller than your fruit or flower shape and glue it to the inside of the card, covering the stitches.

Beads & Blooms

*Send a loved one sparkling wishes
with this whimsical beaded card.*

Designer: **SHARON ROHLOFF**

THE PROJECTS

MATERIALS & TOOLS

- Bone folder
- Yellow card stock,
  8½ x 11 inches (21.6 x 27.9 cm)
- Dotted green paper,
  3½ x 5 inches (8.9 x 12.7 cm)
- Double-sided tape
- Gold embroidery thread,
  20 inches (50.8 cm)
- Patterned glitter paper strip,
  1 x 5½ inches (2.5 x 14 cm)
- Assorted glass beads (4 mm
  pink star, 20 mm white lozenge,
  8 mm green faceted round,
  20 mm amethyst lozenge,
  8 mm turquoise faceted round)
- Beading needle
- Dimensional floral stickers
- Gold pen

STEP BY STEP

1 Fold the yellow card stock in half and smooth with the bone folder. Center and adhere the dotted green paper onto the yellow card stock with double-sided tape.

2 Tape one end of the embroidery thread to the back of the glitter paper strip and wrap the thread around to the front. Add the star bead by using the floss needle to pull the thread through the bead. Wrap the thread around the glitter paper strip until you are back at the front. Add the next bead in the same fashion.

3 Add the third bead in the same way, but wind two more times around the glitter paper strip in varying directions. Wrap the

thread around front and add the next bead.

4 Wrap thread around the strip until you are at the front again. Add the turquoise bead. Wrap once more around the glitter paper strip, secure with tape on the back and cut off the excess thread.

5 Lay the beaded glitter strip on top of the dotted green paper, about 1½ inches (3.8 cm) up from the bottom and use as a guide to affix five sticker flowers above the beaded strip. Draw the stems and spiral leaves with the gold pen on dotted green paper.

6 Tape the beaded glitter strip to the card with double-sided tape 1½ inches (3.8 cm) up from the bottom of the dotted green paper.

Spinning Pretty

These fun beads turn in place with the flick of a finger. Card or toy? You decide!

Designer: **JOAN K. MORRIS**

THE PROJECTS

MATERIALS & TOOLS

- Purple card stock, 5½ x 1½ inches (14 x 3.8 cm)
- Hole punch, ⅝ inch (1.6 cm)
- Purple card stock, 5½ x 2½ inches (14 x 6.4 cm)
- Hole punch, 1 inch (2.5 cm)
- Orange mulberry card stock, 7 inches (17.8 cm) square
- Pencil
- Scissors
- 28-gauge wire
- Wire cutters
- 4 square pearl beads, ⅜ inch (1 cm)
- Clear tape
- Glue stick
- 3 circular pearl beads, ¾ inch (1.9 cm), with hole opening just over ⅜ inch (1 cm)
- 3 green glass flower beads, ⅜ inch (1 cm)

STEP BY STEP

1 Punch four evenly spaced ⅝-inch (1.6 cm) holes in the smaller piece of purple card stock. Punch three evenly spaced 1-inch holes along one side of the larger piece of purple card stock, using the project photo as a guide.

2 Fold the orange mulberry card stock in half, creating a 5 x 7-inch (12.7 x 17.8 cm) card with a side fold.

3 Lay the punched purple pieces in position on the front of the orange folded card using the project photo as a guide. With the pencil, lightly trace the cutout circles onto the orange card.

4 Punch holes into the orange card with the ⅝-inch

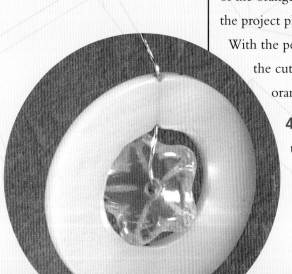

(1.6 cm) hole punch. The 1-inch (2.5 cm) punch will not reach this far into the card, so you must cut the 1-inch (2.5 cm) holes with scissors.

5 Cut four pieces of wire 1¼ inch (3.2 cm) long. Place a small square bead on the wire and tape it in place on the front of the orange card with the wire running horizontally. Glue the punched-out purple card over the orange card, hiding the tape.

6 Cut three pieces of wire 1½ inches (3.8 cm) long. Place the green flower bead inside the round circle bead, stringing them both on the wire, and tape in place on the front of the orange card with the wire running vertically. Glue the punched-out purple card in position over the orange card to hide the tape.

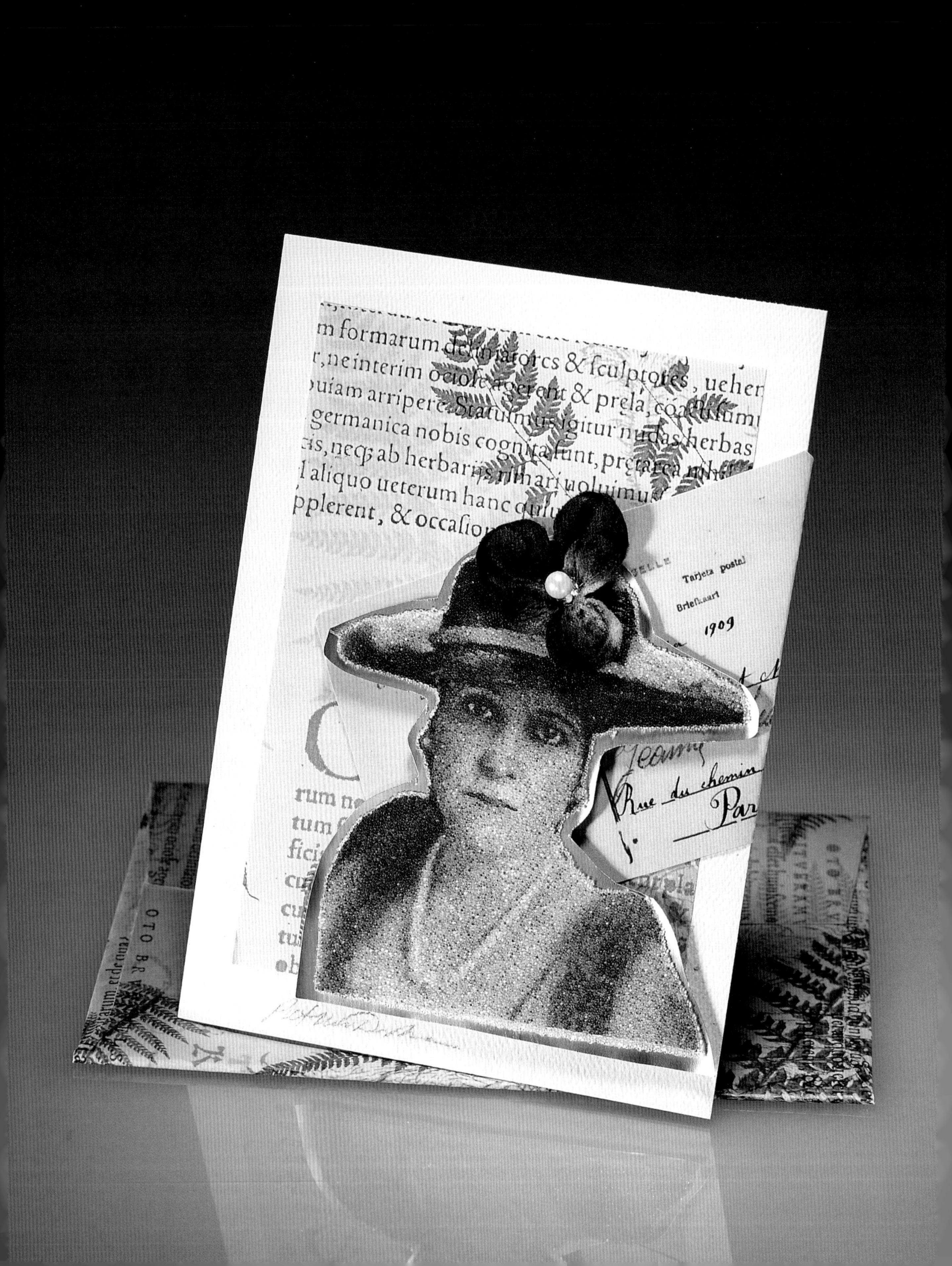

Tarjeta postal
Briefkaart
1909
Rue du chemin

Lavender Lady

Decorate a vintage photo from your family's collection with glass beads to create a keepsake card for the receiver.

Designer: **PATRICIA DiBONA**

MATERIALS & TOOLS

- Off-white watercolor paper, 7 x 10 inches (17.8 x 25.4 cm)
- Scissors
- Bone folder
- Floral paper for background
- Vintage French postcard paper
- Double-sided tape
- Printed photograph on regular paper
- Double-sided sticky paper
- Micro beads, clear glass
- Silver paper
- Foam packing sheet

STEP BY STEP

1 Score and fold the watercolor paper using the bone folder. Cut out a 4 x 6-inch (10.2 x 15.2 cm) sheet of the floral paper.

2 Layer the postcard on top of the background sheet at an angle. Adhere with double-sided tape.

3 Cut out your photograph leaving ⅛ inch (0.3 cm) or more around the image. Cut the sticky paper to roughly fit the photograph's shape.

4 Peel off one layer of plastic from the sticky paper so that one sticky side is exposed. Carefully adhere it to the front of the your photograph. Cut the sticky paper close to the image, making sure there are no edges protruding past the photograph. Peel off the other layer of plastic so that the second sticky side is exposed on top of the photograph.

5 Pour glass micro beads into a shallow box large enough to fit the photograph. Dip the now-sticky front of the photograph into the beads so that they adhere to the sticky paper.

6 Using double-sided tape, adhere your glass–beaded lady to a piece of silver paper. Cut closely around your image to create a soft silver silhouette that will separate your main image from the background images.

7 Cut a piece of foam packing sheet about ½ inch (1.3 cm) smaller than the silver paper and adhere to the back of the silver paper with the tape to give the photograph dimension. Then adhere the photograph layers to the card with double–sided tape.

THE PROJECTS

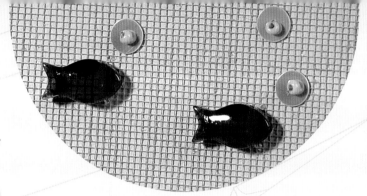

Go Fish!

Dive into beading with the perfect summertime card.

Designer: **CANDIE COOPER**

MATERIALS & TOOLS

- Bone folder
- Mint green card blank, 5½ x 4 inches (14 x 10.2 cm)
- Scissors
- Craft glue
- Aqua mesh, 6 inches (15.2 cm) square
- Textured pink paper, 2 inches (5.1 cm) square
- Tan paper, 4½ x 2 inches (11.4 x 5.1 cm)
- Dark green paper, 2 x 1 inch (5.1 x 2.5 cm)
- Chartreuse paper, 2 inches (5.1 cm) square
- Glue stick
- Needle
- Pink thread
- Pink/orange seed beads
- Orange fish beads, ⅝ x ⅜ inch (1.6 x 1 cm)
- Nylon thread
- 24-gauge wire, 10 inches (25.4 cm)
- Round-nose pliers
- 13 aqua faceted 4 mm glass beads
- Aqua seed beads
- Aqua thread
- Wire cutters

STEP BY STEP

1 Fold the card blank in half, smooth with the bone folder, and cut a wavy edge approximately 1½ inches (3.8 cm) down from the top edge of the card. Paint a thin line of tacky glue at the bottom and side edges and along the top wavy edge. Lay the aqua mesh over the card front and press down. Set it aside until the glue has dried.

2 Cut out a coral shape from the pink paper. Cut out a sea floor from the tan paper.

3 Cut three skinny wavy strips of dark green paper for the lines on the green plant. With the glue stick, adhere two pieces in a "V" shape and one by itself onto the chartreuse paper. Using the photo as a guide, cut around the "V" shape—this will be the front plant piece. Cut out the single dark green strip, which will go behind the "V."

4 Cut away the excess aqua mesh, but leave an extra ⅛-inch (0.3 cm) border above the wavy edge.

5 Glue the sand piece down at the bottom edge of the card, followed by the coral and the green plant.

6 Thread your needle with the pink thread. Poke holes through the card where you want the seed beads placed on the coral. Bring the needle through to the front of the card and string one seed bead. Put the needle back through and out through the next hole and seed bead. Continue until all the seed beads have been connected. Tie off the thread at the back and trim away the excess, adding a dot of glue

where the thread ends. Add fish and bubbles in the same way with clear nylon thread.

7 Make a tiny curl at the end of the wire with pliers and string one aqua glass bead followed by three seed beads, repeating this sequence until you have used all the aqua glass beads. Bend the beaded wire so it follows the wave line and finish the end of the wire with another tiny loop.

With the aqua thread and needle, stitch the wire loop to the card. Stitch the last loop to the card and tie off the thread on the back. Seal the thread with a dot of glue.

Straight from the Heart

Your nearest and dearest will feel the love when they receive this affectionate card.

Designer: **CANDIE COOPER**

MATERIALS & TOOLS

- 2 pink card blanks, 5½ x 4¼ inches (14 x 10.8 cm)
- Scissors
- Gold and white paper, 4 x 3¼ inches (10.2 x 8.3 cm)
- Glue stick
- Gold paper, 4½ x 1 inch (11.4 x 2.5 cm)
- Eyelet hole punch
- Eyelet setting tool
- Self-healing mat
- Mallet
- 4 brass eyelets, ⅛ inch
- Washi paper to match card
- Pencil
- Plastic laminator
- Plastic laminating sleeves
- Hole punch, 1/16 inch
- 26-gauge wire, 15 inches (38.1 cm) long
- Round-nose pliers
- Pink and white seed bead mix
- Wire cutters
- Foam stickers, ⅜ inch (1 cm) in diameter
- Ribbon to match card, 1½ x ¾ inch (3.8 x 1.9 cm)
- Fabric glue
- Paper clip

STEP BY STEP

1 Cut one pink card blank so it measures 4½ x 4¼ inches (11.4 x 10.8 cm). Cut ⅜ inch (1 cm) off the bottom front edge (opposite the folded edge).

2 Glue the gold and white paper square to the front center of the card. With glue stick, adhere the gold piece of paper to the bottom inside edge of the card. Fold the excess over to the back side and glue.

3 Use the eyelet hole punch to cut a hole in each of the four corners of the gold and white paper. Thread a brass eyelet through the paper and set with the eyelet setter.

4 Draw a heart pattern onto the Washi paper and cut it out. Glue the Washi heart to the extra pink card blank and cut out, leaving a small border. Laminate the heart piece and trim away excess laminate.

5 Punch small holes around the border of the heart with the hole punch. Make a loop at one end of the wire with the round-nose pliers. Thread the wire through one of the holes from the back to the front. String one pink, one white, and one pink seed bead onto the wire and put the tail around to the back and through the next hole. This time string the beads white, pink, white onto the wire and through the next hole. Continue until you return to where you started. Thread the tail of the wire through the starting loop and lock the wires into place. Trim away excess wire with the wire cutters.

6 Place three foam stickers on the back of the heart and stick in the middle of the card. Add a line of fabric glue to the end of the piece of ribbon. Fold it so the two ends meet up and clip so the ends stay together until they dry. Add another line of glue at the top of the ribbon and stick to the inside bottom edge of the card to create a tab.

7 Cut four small hearts from the Washi paper and glue on the inside corners of the card so the paper shows through the eyelet holes.

Bollywood Cards

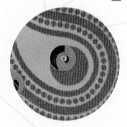

Paisley—a traditional pattern in India—is given an oh-so-modern touch with this bright pink and flocked paper. Bedecked with lively ribbon, vintage sequins, and seed beads, these cards are a cinematic treat.

Designer: **TERRY TAYLOR**

MATERIALS & TOOLS

- Scissors
- Card stock
- Decorative paper
- Spray adhesive
- Bone folder
- Craft glue
- Ribbon
- Sequins
- Sewing needle
- Invisible sewing thread
- Cellophane tape
- Seed beads

STEP BY STEP

1 Determine the size of your finished card. Cut a piece of card stock to the dimensions you desire.

2 Cut a piece of decorative paper slightly small than your card stock. Adhere it to the card stock with the spray adhesive. When dry, fold the card and smooth with a bone folder.

3 Use the craft glue to adhere the ribbon to the card as desired. Use a small amount of glue to fix each sequin to the card. Allow the glue to dry.

4 Use a needle to prick the card stock in the middle of each sequin.

5 Thread the needle with a length of invisible thread. Anchor the thread to the back of the card with a small piece of tape. Stitch a seed bead to each sequin. If additional beads or sequins are desired, prick the card stock with the needle and stitch each in place.

6 Finish the card by gluing a piece of decorative paper on the inside of the card to hide the stitching thread.

Bird & Berries Card

The use of wire as a threading tool gives the beads a three-dimensional effect. Hand carve your own rubber stamp to individualize your hungry bird.

Designer: **SUSAN McBRIDE**

THE PROJECTS

MATERIALS & TOOLS

- Blank card made of brown craft paper
- Brayer
- Paintbrush
- Acrylic paint
- Hand-carved stamp or store-bought bird stamp, about 3 x 3½ inches (7.6 x 8.9 cm)
- Stamping ink
- Mulberry paper
- Scissors
- Decoupage medium
- Brush for glue
- Wire cutters
- Thin wire
- Variety of red glass beads
- Needle

■ STEP BY STEP

1 Lay the card out flat and paint a background. The designer used green, blue, and orange acrylic paint, layering her color with both a paintbrush and a brayer. You may want to experiment with these processes on scrap paper before making your final card.

2 Ink your stamp using a brayer or a stamping pad, and press the inked stamp onto a piece of mulberry paper. Mulberry paper is very thin, but strong; it has an excellent surface for stamping. When the image has dried, cut it out and, using decoupage medium and a brush, glue it to the front of your painted card. Smooth out any wrinkles and allow it to dry.

3 Cut 10 inches (25.4 cm) of thin wire. Thread a red bead onto the wire and then pass the wire through the bead once again to secure. Thread as many red beads as you desire and twist the wire to resemble a vine.

TS

THE PROJECTS

4 With a needle, poke a small hole into the front of the card. Insert one end of the wire. Knot or twist the wire on the opposite side of the card so that it will stay secure. Do the same thing on the other side of the wire, being sure to keep the kinks and twists in the wire so it looks like a vine.

5 Using the process described in step 4, put a berry in the bird's beak and a few berries in the background. If you mail this card, send it in a padded envelope to protect it from damage.

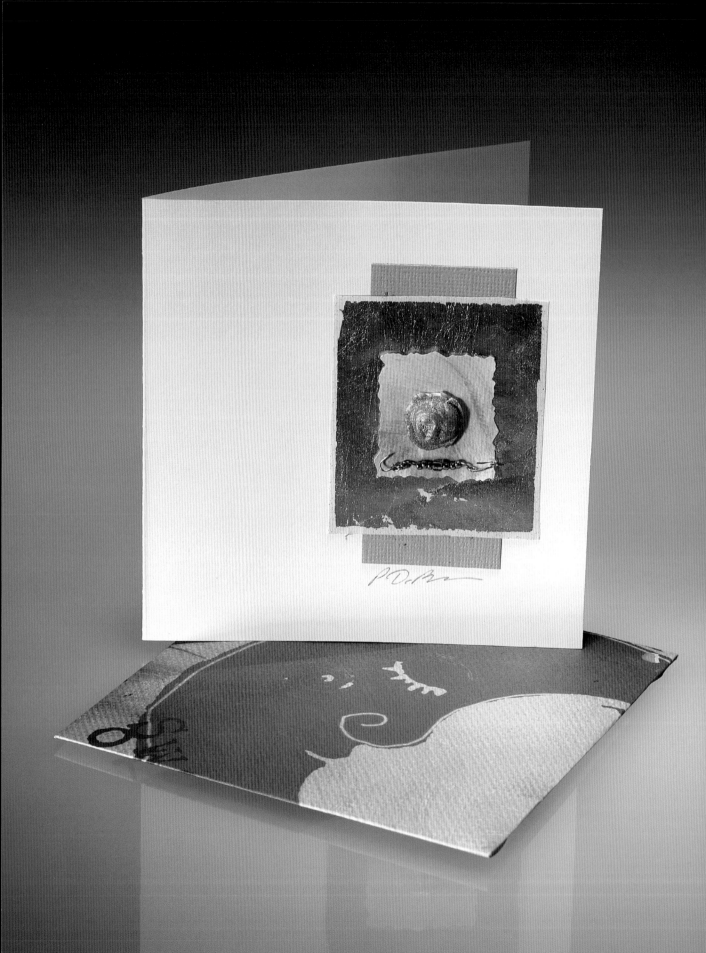

Moon Beam

The sleepy clay moon on this card will inspire sweet dreams.

Designer: **PATRICIA DiBONA**

MATERIALS & TOOLS

- Air-dry clay
- Small moon face mold
- Gold metallic paint
- Adhesive glaze
- Scissors
- White card stock 9⁹⁄₁₆ x 4⁷⁄₈ inches (24.3 x 12.4 cm)
- Bone folder
- Double-sided tape
- Textured lavender paper, 1½ x 3⁵⁄₁₆ inches (3.8 cm x 8.4 cm)
- Gold-foiled paper, 2¹¹⁄₁₆ x 2¼ inches (6.8 x 5.7 cm)
- Hand-painted paper, 1¼ x 1⅜ inches (3.2 x 3.5 cm)
- 8 seed beads
- 26-gauge copper wire, 2½ inches (6.4 cm) long
- Jewelry glue

■ STEP BY STEP

1 Lightly press a thumbful of clay into the mold. Scrape off the excess and remove carefully. Let the clay dry overnight and then paint it gold. Once the paint is dry, seal it with adhesive glaze.

2 Score and fold the white card stock with the bone folder.

3 Use double-sided tape to adhere the textured paper 2½ inches (6.4 cm) from the card fold and 1 inch (2.5 cm) from the bottom. Center the gold foil on the textured lavender paper, and center the hand-painted paper on the gold foil and secure it with double-sided tape.

4 Use adhesive glaze to adhere the clay moon face in the middle of the painted paper.

5 String the seed beads through the wire, tie off the ends, and glue to the card with jewelry glue.

Sweet & Lovely

This delightful card is perfect for Mother's Day or Valentine's Day.

Designer: **SHARON ROHLOFF**

MATERIALS & TOOLS

- Light pink card stock, 8½ x 11 inches (21.6 x 27.9 cm)
- Large-scale floral paper, 3¾ x 4¾ inches (9.5 x 12 cm)
- Decorative scissors
- Double-sided tape
- Green/pink striped paper, ½ x 5½ inches (1.3 x 14 cm)
- Green houndstooth paper, 1⅜ x 5½ inches (4.1 x 14 cm)
- Glue
- Narrow pink ribbon, 5½ inches (14 cm) long
- Medium pink card stock, 2 inches (5.1 cm) square
- "Love" circle stamp
- Embossing ink
- Gold embossing powder
- Pink felt pen
- Heat gun (optional)
- Scissors
- Dark pink card stock, 2½ x 1⅜ inches (6.4 x 3.5 cm)
- Gold pen
- 2 gold eyelets
- 34-gauge gold wire, 4½ inches (11.4 cm) long
- 4 metallic gold/pink glass beads, 3 mm
- 2 crystal beads, 6 mm
- 1 olive green bicone, 3 mm
- 1 pale pink faceted round, 6 mm
- Wire cutters
- 2 foam dots

■ STEP BY STEP

1 Fold the pink card stock in half. Cut a 3¾ x 5-inch (9.5 x 12.7 cm) rectangle from floral paper with decorative scissors. Center and adhere to pink card stock with double-sided tape.

2 Center and adhere the striped paper on top of the houndstooth print paper with double-sided tape. Glue the ribbon down the center of the striped paper. Tape the houndstooth band ¾ inches (1.9 cm) up from the base of the card with double-sided tape.

3 Stamp the medium pink paper and emboss with gold embossing powder. Darken the petals of the embossed design with the pink felt pen. Cut out the stamped design after it dries, or use a heat gun to dry the powder.

4 Cut a 2½ x 1⅜-inch (6.4 x 3.5 cm) rectangle from dark pink card stock and use decorative scissors to trim the short sides. Gild edges with gold pen. Inset two gold eyelets 1 inch (2.5 cm)

apart and ½ inch (1.3 cm) up from the bottom of the scalloped edge. Adhere the embossed stamp ⅛ inch (0.3 cm) down from the top of the scalloped edge with double-sided tape.

5 Thread the gold wire through the beads and center them on the wire. Thread your wire ends through eyelets so the beads lie flat. Twist the ends of the wire together on the back of the pink rectangle, trim off any excess wire, and press flat.

6 Glue the foam dots to the back top and bottom of the small pink rectangle. Adhere the rectangle to the card with glue, slightly off center to the right on top of the other decorative papers.

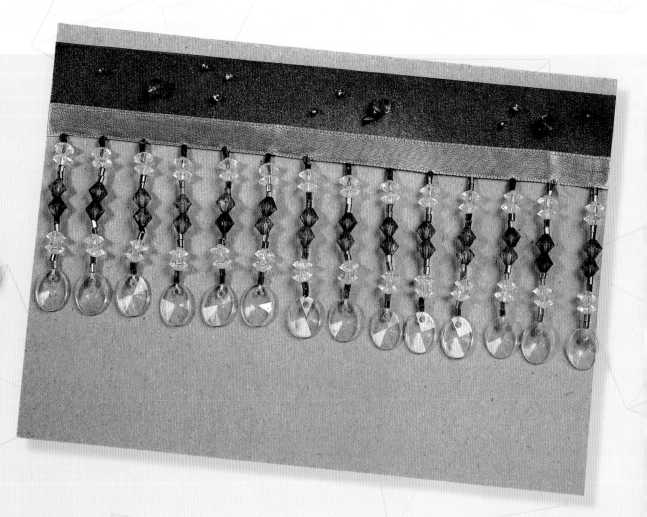

On the Fringe

People will think you spent hours crafting this card. The secret? Pre-strung beaded fringe! All you need to do is glue it down.

Designer: **NICOLE McCONVILLE**

MATERIALS & TOOLS

- Clear-drying craft glue
- Small glue brush
- Card stock in coordinating color, 1 x 7 inches (2.5 x 17.8 cm)
- Blank card, 5 x 7 inches (12.7 x 17.8 cm)
- Beaded fringe, approximately 9 inches (22.9 cm) long
- Scissors
- Beading thread
- Beading needle

■ STEP BY STEP

1 Brush a thin layer of glue along the backside of the strip of card stock. Press down onto the card front, approximately ⅛ inch (0.3 cm) in from the folded edge. Set aside to dry.

2 Carefully brush a thin layer of glue along the backside of the beaded fridge ribbon. Press onto the front of the card with your fingers, along the edge of the strip of card stock. There will be an inch of fringe hanging off each side of the card.

3 Snip off the beads from the fringe hanging off the edges of the card. This will allow the flat ribbon surface to adhere to the inside of the card for a clean look. Simply brush glue along the backside of that ribbon, and fold over into the inside cover of the card. Press down with your fingers and set aside to dry.

4 If you desire further embellishment, snip off some extra beads from your leftover beaded fringe. Stitch them onto the card stock strip in a random pattern.

83

All Four Love

The glass-bead covering on this card seals in your love.
Send it out, and it may come back tenfold!

Designer: **PATRICIA DiBONA**

MATERIALS & TOOLS

- Off-white watercolor paper, 7 x 10 inches (17.8 x 25.4 cm)
- Bone folder
- Scissors
- Green decorative paper
- Silver scalloped trim
- White glue
- Double-sided tape
- "Love" rubber stamp or other rubber stamp image
- Card stock
- Silver paper
- Micro beads, clear glass
- Foam packing sheet

■ STEP BY STEP

1 Score and fold the watercolor paper using the bone folder. Cut out a 6 x 4-inch (15.2 x 10.2 cm) sheet of the green paper. Adhere the silver trim to one side of the green background with a small amount of glue and adhere the green background sheet to the card with double-sided tape.

2 Stamp your "Love" or other rubber stamp image onto card stock and cut out, then cut out a slightly larger square of silver paper as a background to the rubber stamp image.

3 Adhere the glass beads to the stamped image using the instructions listed in steps 3 to 5 on page 69.

4 Cut out a square of packing sheet slightly smaller than your bead-coated rubber stamp image. Adhere this to the back of the rubber stamp image with double-sided tape. Then, adhere these two layers to the silver paper with the tape, and finally adhere the silver paper, the foam, and the rubber stamp image to the card with the double-sided tape. Slightly offset the silver paper from the green background paper.

Desert Vessel

Elements of copper and viridian lend a masculine flare to this Southwest-themed card.

Designer: **SUSAN MOSTEK**

MATERIALS & TOOLS

- Southwest jar stamp
- Decorative background paper
- Extra brown card stock for layering and stamping
- Clear pigment ink
- Black embossing powder
- Heat gun
- Scissors
- Copper metallic paint pen
- Foam tape
- Copper wire
- 3 metallic iridescent beads
- Brown card stock, folded to 5⅜ x 5 inches (13.7 x 12.7 cm)
- Double-sided tape
- Paper cutter (optional)
- Black card stock
- Copper metallic paper

THE PROJECTS

▇ STEP BY STEP

1 Stamp the Southwest jar twice, once onto decorative background paper and again onto a scrap of brown card stock, using the clear pigment ink. Sprinkle the ink with black embossing powder. Heat emboss with the heat gun and cut the jar out of metallic paper and the feathers from the brown card stock scrap.

2 Color lines on the jar with the copper metallic paint pen. Attach the brown feathers with small pieces of foam tape. Wrap the copper wire around neck of jar, wrapping wire around spines of feathers and adding three iridescent beads as you go.

3 Attach the jar to a 3¼ x 2⅞-inch (8.3 x 7.3 cm) piece of brown card stock using small cut pieces of foam tape.

4 With the double-sided tape, attach the brown card stock to a slightly larger piece of black card stock. Continue layering, starting with a 4⅜ x 4-inch (11.1 x 10.2 cm) piece of decorative paper, then a slightly larger piece of copper metallic card stock, to a black card stock piece and finally the folded brown card.

Honey Beads

Vintage plastic flower beads inspired these cards. The commercially made Asian paper notecards were paired with other handmade papers.

Designer: **TERRY TAYLOR**

MATERIALS & TOOLS

- Decorative punches
- Scissors
- Asian handmade papers
- Gold decorative papers
- Notecards
- Craft glue
- Needle
- Invisible sewing thread
- Plastic flower beads
- Small gold-plated beads

■ STEP BY STEP

1 Create flower and circle shapes from Asian and gold papers with decorative punches or scissors. In this project, gold-printed black paper and saffron-colored handmade paper were used to create circular and floral shapes. Glue the shapes to the notecards as desired.

2 Thread the needle with invisible thread. Stitch each flower bead to the card, securing them with gold-plated beads.

3 Cut out decorative paper slightly smaller than the stitched areas of your card. Adhere the paper to the inside front of the card to hide the stitching. In this project, strips of the gold-printed black paper were used to hide the stitches.

Graphic Overlap

Pile on the paper! Bold colors and patterns complement each other on this card.

Designer: **JOAN K. MORRIS**

■ MATERIALS & TOOLS

- Graphic circle paper, 2 x 5½ inches (5.1 x 14 cm)
- Orange seed beads
- Turquoise seed beads
- Black sewing thread
- Beading needle
- Two-tone graphic floral paper, 2½ x 6½ inches (6.4 x 16.5 cm)
- Glue stick
- Two-tone graphic dotted paper, 7 inches (17.8 cm) square
- White card stock, 7 inches (17.8 cm) square

■ STEP BY STEP

1 On the graphic circle paper, stitch the seed beads in place using the needle and thread, placing one bead per stitch. Place the beads over matching colors around the circle and fill in some of the circle centers. Tie a knot on the back side every five or six beads in case the thread breaks.

2 Center the beaded paper onto the graphic floral paper. Glue with the glue stick.

3 Stitch beads in the flower centers around the edge of the floral paper.

4 Fold the 7-inch-square (17.8 cm) graphic paper in half to create a 3½ x 7-inch (8.9 x 17.8 cm) card with a side fold.

5 Center and glue the two beaded pieces of paper on the front of the folded paper. Stitch beads in place on the edge of the folded paper following some of the design.

6 Fold the 7-inch-square (17.8 cm) piece of white card stock in half and glue it to the inside of the folded beaded paper.

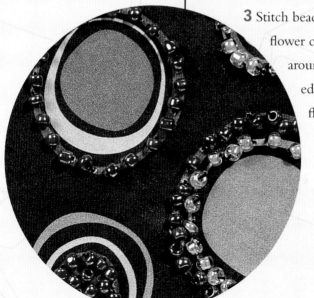

A Little Bird Told Me

Fluttering green leaves and a sweetly singing bird welcome spring. Create interesting new bird species with a variety of Japanese Washi papers.

Designer: **CANDIE COOPER**

MATERIALS & TOOLS

- Brown paper, 6 x 3 inches (15.2 x 7.6 cm)
- Scissors
- Craft glue
- Blue card blank, 5½ x 4¼ inches (14 x 10.8 cm)
- Sewing machine
- Brown thread
- Orange/coral Washi paper, 3 inches (7.6 cm) square
- Sheet music, 2 inches (5.2 cm) square
- Orange paper, ½ inch (1.3 cm) square
- Pink tulle, 2 inches (5.2 cm) square
- Orange/coral seed beads
- Sewing needle
- Pink thread
- Green fabric, 3 inches (7.6 cm) square
- Green sewing thread
- 9 pressed glass green leaf beads, 9 mm
- Green seed beads
- Foam sticker, ⅜ inch (1 cm) in diameter
- Eyelet hole punch
- Mallet
- Eyelet setting tool
- Silver eyelet, 1/16 inch (2 mm)

STEP BY STEP

1 Cut out the brown paper in the shape of a branch. Glue this piece just below the horizontal center of the card and leave to dry. Use the sewing machine to straight stitch a border around the card, stitching on top of the branch.

2 Draw a bird pattern on the Washi paper and a wing on the sheet music and cut both out. Cut a small triangle from the orange paper for the bird's beak.

3 Paint a thin layer of glue on top of the wing and place the tulle over it. Once the glue has dried, cut away the excess tulle. Bringing a threaded needle from the back to the front, slide a seed bead onto the needle and poke the needle back through the same hole it came through. Repeat for desired number of beads. When you are satisfied, trim the thread leaving a 1-inch (2.5 cm) tail on the backside of the wing. Glue it down securely.

4 Cut nine heart-shaped leaves from the green fabric so they are a little bigger than the leaf beads. Glue the fabric leaves on top of the branch. Add a dot of glue to attach a glass leaf bead to the top of a fabric leaf. Repeat for the remaining leaves and leave to dry.

5 Thread the needle with green thread and string a seed bead onto the needle. Put the needle down through a leaf bead to the back of the card and back up just next to the leaf bead. Tie the two ends in a knot and trim, leaving two small tails. Repeat for the remaining leaves.

6 Glue the bird on top of the branch. Place the foam sticker on the middle of the back of the wing. Add a small dot of glue to the end of the wing closest to the bird's head and stick into place. Cut three ⅜-inch-long (1 cm) strips from the sheet music and glue onto the tail. Glue the beak into place. Use the eyelet setting tool to cut a place for the eye. Thread the silver eyelet through the two layers of paper and set.

Wire Whimsy Tags

These bead and wire characters can be easily personalized by creating different poses and surroundings.

Designer: **DEBBIE CRANE**

MATERIALS & TOOLS

- Pencil
- Ruler
- Card stock, 2½ x 4 inches (6.4 x 10.2 cm)
- Scissors
- Hole punch
- 8 inches (20.3 cm) narrow ribbon
- 26-gauge wire, 9 inches (22.9 cm)
- Wire cutters
- Large, flat bead for body, 1 inch (2.5 cm) tall
- Needle-nose pliers
- Craft glue
- Black fine point marker
- Assorted 2 mm beads

■ STEP BY STEP

1 Trace a tag shape onto card stock and cut out the tag. Punch a hole at the narrow end and thread the ribbon through the hole.

2 Cut the wire into two pieces, 6 inches (15.2 cm) and 3 inches (7.6 cm) long. Bend the 6-inch (15.2 cm) wire into almost half and feed the ends through the hole in the center of the large, flat bead, keeping a loop outside.

3 Use the loop to create a head by twisting three times to make a neck. The two ends coming out of the bottom of the bead will become legs. Bend and cut the legs to your desired pose. Use the needle-nose pliers to make small loops for the feet.

4 Twist the 3-inch (7.6 cm) length of wire around the neck to make arms. Bend and cut as desired. Use the pliers to make small loops for the hands.

5 Use craft glue to attach the bead body to the front of the tag. Create flowers, butterflies, or stars by drawing a small doodle with the black marker and accenting it with small, glued-on beads.

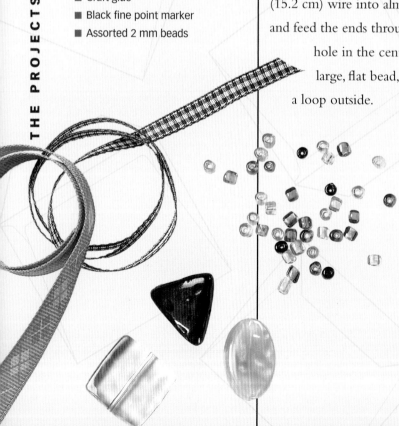

Blazing Sunflower

The shimmering beads mimic sunflower seeds on this cheery, warm-toned card.

Designer: **JEAN TOMASO MOORE**

MATERIALS & TOOLS

- Card stock
- Bone folder
- Silk or fabric flowers
- Scissors
- Various decorative papers
- Double-sided tape
- Craft glue
- 32-gauge beading wire
- Wire cutters
- Beading needle
- Brown 2 mm beads
- Cellophane tape
- Pliers (any type)
- Red 10 x 5 mm rectangle beads

■ STEP BY STEP

1 Fold the card stock and smooth with the bone folder. Remove the plastic center from your silk or fabric flowers. Cut out various background papers to add color and texture to the card. Use double-sided tape to adhere the papers to the card. Here, the designer used two blocks of paper with an orange and yellow print.

2 Glue the flower petals to the card on top of the decorative paper. Poke a hole through the center of the flower.

Use a variety of silk flowers, beads, and decorative papers for a totally different look.

3 Thread the small brown beads onto the beading wire. Push the beaded wire through the hole in the center of the flower and use cellophane tape to hold the tail of the wire in place on the inside of the card. Wrap extra wire around the beads with pliers on the front of the card to secure them.

4 Thread the red beads onto the beading wire and stitch six beads around the brown beads. Add red beads to the bottom of the card. If you prefer not to use wire to attach your beads, you can use glue to adhere the beads to the card.

5 To finish, cut a piece of card stock to fit inside the card. Use double-sided tape or glue to adhere the card stock to the inside of card to cover the exposed wire.

The Road Traveled

Share your memories with others by collecting found papers
from your next travel adventure to use for this card.

Designer: **KIM GRANT**

MATERIALS & TOOLS

- Piece of card stock, 5½ x 8½ inch (14 x 21.6 cm)
- Bone folder
- Envelope, 4½ x 5¾ inch (11.4 x 14.6 cm)
- Joss paper
- Local newspaper
- Paper money
- Found papers collected on your trip
- Steel-edged ruler
- Glue stick
- Faux postage rubber stamps
- Black stamp pad
- Spiral rubber stamp
- Gold stamp pad
- Glitter glue
- Hole punch
- Metallic threads
- Beads or found objects

■ STEP BY STEP

1 Fold the card stock in half and smooth with a bone folder. Tear various-sized pieces from your stash of collected papers. Don't use scissors; tear using a metal edge ruler for a softer edge on your collage.

2 Glue the papers onto the card stock with a glue stick, overlapping the paper where you like. Rubber-stamp the faux postage stamp images onto the card using black ink. Rubber-

stamp a larger image onto the card using gold ink. This project's designer used a gold spiral design.

3 Add glitter glue designs in small amounts. Let everything dry.

4 Punch two holes onto edge of card and pull metallic thread through the holes.

5 Attach beads onto the dangling thread or glue random beads onto the card. Embellish your envelope repeating the same techniques. For a variation, sew foreign currency onto the card as you would beads.

Heartfelt Portraits

This card says a thousand words. Alternate photographs in the frame for different occasions.

Designer: **CANDIE COOPER**

MATERIALS & TOOLS

- Card blank
- Scissors
- 1 sheet red craft felt
- Fabric glue
- 1 sheet purple craft felt
- 1 sheet clear plastic
- Pinking shears
- Sewing machine
- Felt circles, ⅜ inches (1 cm) in diameter
- Sunburst-shaped sequins
- Sewing needle
- Red thread
- 1/0 multi-colored seed beads
- Multi-purpose adhesive
- 1/0 clear seed beads

■ STEP BY STEP

1 Cut out the card blank so that, when glued to the red felt, there will be a ⅜- to ½-inch (1 to 1.3 cm) border of felt around the card. Glue the card to the felt.

2 Cut a rectangle shape out of the purple felt and plastic to fit the photo size, adding a little extra room to account for trimming around the photo with pinking shears. Machine-stitch the plastic to the purple felt on three sides, leaving a little extra room to trim around the border with pinking shears.

3 Place a line of fabric glue around the back of the purple felt piece and glue to the front center of the red card.

4 Glue a felt circle to the center of each of the sequins and leave to dry. Thread the sewing needle with red thread. Double the thread over and knot it at the end. Bring the needle up through the back of the sequin, through the felt circle and a seed bead. Put the needle

back through the felt and sequin, tie off the thread and trim. Repeat six more times, for the remaining sequin embellishments.

5 Glue the sequin embellishments to the opposite corners of the plastic photo sleeve with multipurpose adhesive and leave to dry.

6 With the same needle and thread, anchor your stitches on the back of the red felt and stitch clear seed beads around the border of the card. Anchor your thread as you did when you started and trim away the excess.

7 After everything dries, slip in a photo of your choice.

Beady Bubbles

Rings of beads against a sunshine background will brighten anyone's day.

Designer: **CANDIE COOPER**

MATERIALS

- 4 paper circles, each 1½ inches (3.8 cm) in diameter
- Card blank, 5½ x 4½ inches (14 x 11.4 cm)
- Glue stick
- Nylon cording
- Seed bead variety mix
- Variety of 3 mm faceted beads
- 26-gauge wire
- Sewing needle
- Thread to match card
- Craft glue
- Sequin mix

■ STEP BY STEP

1 Arrange the four paper circles on the front of the card and glue into place with a glue stick.

2 String the desired number of beads in a variety of sequences onto the nylon cord. Tie the two ends together to make a beaded ring. Repeat in different patterns, sizes, and colors.

3 String the seed beads onto the 26-gauge wire. When you are finished stringing, thread one tail through five beads in the opposite direction from the other wire. Pull the two ends away from each other to tighten the beaded ring.

4 Place the beaded rings on top of the paper circles. Poke holes through the card with the needle close to the inside and outside of the beaded loops—this is where the stitches will go. Do this at three points around each of the beaded rings.

5 Thread the needle and poke it through the card from back to front next to a beaded loop and back down on the opposite side and repeat in the same spot. Continue stitching the beaded loops to the front of the card. When you are finished, tie off your thread on the back of the card and secure with a dot of glue.

6 Fill in vacant areas inside the bead rings with sequins. Glue each sequin to the card inside the bead rings with craft glue. Thread the needle as you did before and bring it through a sequin from the back of the card. String one seed bead onto the needle and poke it back through the hole in the sequin. Repeat for the remaining sequins and when finished, anchor the thread as you did before with glue.

Silk Road

Make an elegant statement with subtly shimmering silks.

Designer: **CANDIE COOPER**

THE PROJECTS

MATERIALS

- Silk fabric
- Card blank, 6¼ x 4½ inches (15.9 x 11.4 cm)
- Scissors
- Fabric glue
- Paintbrush
- Decorative paper
- Cream textured paper
- 3 pieces of beading wire, each 9 inches (22.9 cm) long
- #2 gold crimp beads
- Chain-nose pliers
- Beads to match silk and paper
- Seed beads to match silk and paper
- Sewing pins
- Self-healing mat
- Eyelet hole punch
- 6 bronze eyelets, ⅛ inch (0.3 cm)
- Eyelet setting tool
- Mallet
- Wire cutters

■ STEP BY STEP

1 Cut a piece of silk to fit the front side of the card. Fray the edges by pulling away some of the threads around the border. Trim slightly with scissors, leaving some raveling threads. Paint a thin layer of fabric glue on the front side of the card and adhere the fabric.

2 Cut a rectangle from the decorative paper measuring 5½ x 3½ inches (14 x 8.9 cm) and glue it into the center of the card on top of the fabric.

3 Cut the cream colored paper so it measures 5¾ x 2¼ inches (14.6 x 5.7 cm). Glue the cream paper strip on top of the decorative paper down the middle of the card.

4 String one crimp bead 1¼ inches (3.2 cm) down the wire and flatten it with the chain nose pliers. String short sequences of beads onto the beading wire, separating each sequence with crimp beads. Leave a little wire showing between the beaded sections.

5 Lay the three finished wires down the center of the card. Mark the six eyelet placements at the end of each wire with pins. Open the card and place on a self-healing mat. Cut each of the holes for the eyelets with an eyelet hole punch. Poke each of the eyelets through the silk and card and set.

6 Thread the tail of wire through the corresponding eyelet to the inside of the card. Turn the card over and string a crimp bead onto the wire and flatten with the chain-nose pliers. Repeat for the opposite end of the wire, pulling the wire snug before crimping. Repeat for the remaining wires and trim away excess wire with wire cutters.

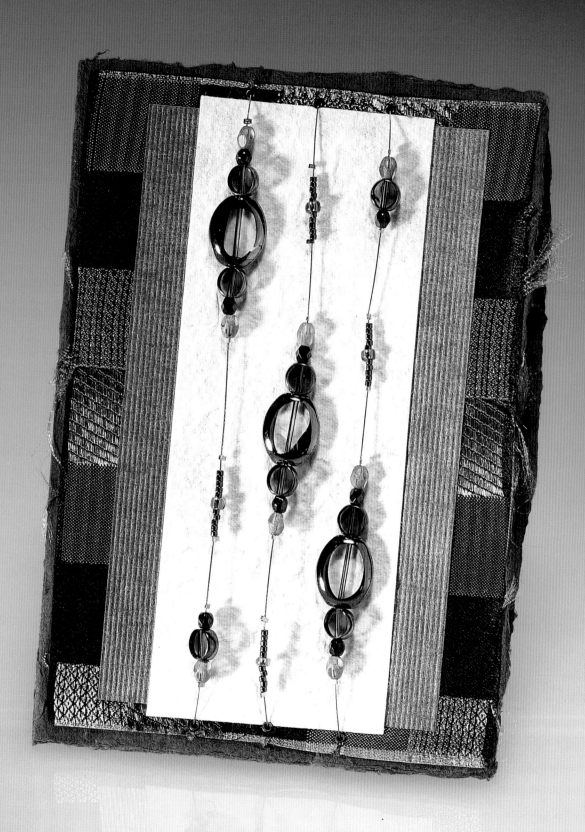

Doodle Heart Card

Love may be complicated, but you'll find this creation refreshingly simple to make.

Designer: **ELIZABETH BECK**

MATERIALS

- Scrap paper and pencil
- White watercolor paper
- Black permanent pen
- Scissors
- Several red glass beads, 4 mm
- Beading needle
- White or red thread
- Red card stock, 12 x 6 inches (30.5 x 15.2 cm)
- Glue stick or craft glue

◾ STEP BY STEP

1 On a piece of scrap paper, draw a heart shape and cut it out. The heart has no size requirement: It can be as tall, as skinny, or as lopsided and character-filled as you'd like. Trace your heart shape onto a piece of watercolor paper lightly with a pencil.

2 Fill the heart with doodles using the permanent black pen. Here, loopy scrolls are used to fill the heart. Start with the outside edge of your heart and scroll inwards. Erase any pencil marks that aren't drawn over.

3 Cut out the heart with a ¼-inch (0.6 cm) border beyond your doodling.

4 Pick out small glass beads to match your card stock. Here, a deep red was used. Your thread can match your beads or your white watercolor paper.

5 Sew the glass beads onto the heart, starting from back to front and beading one bead per stitch. You can use thread to match either the heart or the beads. Scatter them randomly throughout the doodle.

6 Glue your doodled and beaded heart onto card stock.

Letter Perfect

Add a personal touch with a monogrammed card created for someone special.

Designer: **BRANDY LOGAN**

THE PROJECTS

MATERIALS

- Glue stick or craft glue
- Die-cut letter
- Solid-colored card stock, 4½ x 5½ inches (11.4 x 14 cm)
- Black pen
- Glass beads
- 26-gauge wire
- Decorative charm
- Cellophane tape
- Stripe patterned paper, 3¾ x 4¾ inches (9.5 x 12 cm)
- Burnished card stock, 4¾ x 11 inches (12 x 27.9 cm)
- Foam sticker dots
- Needle (optional)
- Colored floss (optional)

▪ STEP BY STEP

1 Glue the die-cut letter to the solid-colored card stock. Trace the letter with black pen and draw a defining line near the edges of the solid-colored card stock.

2 Thread four beads onto the wire, then thread the charm, and then four more beads.

3 Push the wire ends through both sides of the first stroke of the letter, piercing through the colored card stock. Tape the ends down on the backside of the card stock.

4 Glue the colored card stock onto the striped paper.

5 Fold the burnished card stock in half. Glue the striped paper to the front of the card using foam sticker dots.

6 To further decorate this card, you can sew an "X" pattern randomly around the edges of the colored card stock using colored floss.

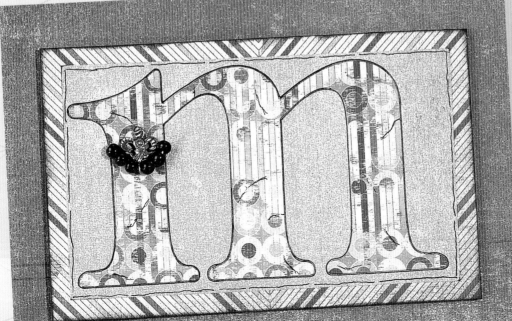

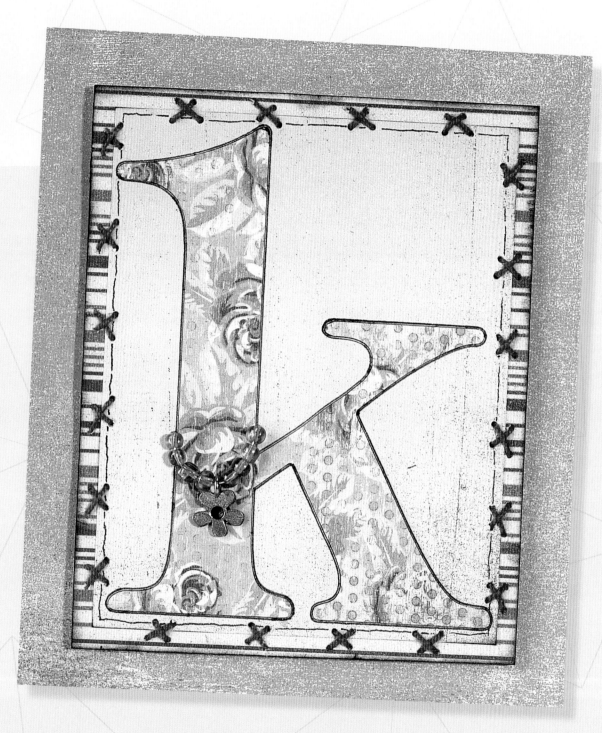

Snowglobe Card

White seed beads become a snowstorm of good wishes with a little clear vinyl and a few stitches.

Designer: **DEBBIE CRANE**

MATERIALS

- Light blue card stock, 4½ x 3 inches (11.4 x 7.6 cm)
- Red card stock, folded to 5½ x 4 inches (14 x 10.2 cm)
- Glue stick
- Pencil
- White and red construction paper
- Scissors
- Clear vinyl, 4½ x 3 inches (11.4 x 7.6 cm)
- Sewing machine
- Black thread
- White seed beads

STEP BY STEP

1 Glue the light blue card stock to the center of the red card.

2 Trace a snowman and scarf shape onto construction paper and cut out. Assemble the snowman and glue to the lower center of the light blue card stock.

3 Machine- or tightly hand-stitch the vinyl over the light blue card stock on three sides.

4 Add beads inside the opening at the top, and sew that side shut.

If you'd like to cover your stitches, adhere a strip of blue card stock to the inside front cover of the card.

Blooming Ribbons

A bright and casual way to cheer up someone's day, this pastel card is blossoming with sweet simplicity.

Designer: **JOAN K. MORRIS**

THE PROJECTS

MATERIALS

- Pastel card stock, 3¼ inches (8.3 cm) square
- Hole punch, ⅛ inch (0.3 cm)
- 3 yards of ribbon, ⅛ inch (0.3 cm) wide
- Scissors
- Sewing needle: Eye should be large enough to thread the ribbon, but small enough to go through the beads
- 3 assorted colors of size "E" beads
- Pencil
- Complementary pastel card stock, 4 x 8 inches (10.2 x 20.3 cm)
- Glue stick

■ STEP BY STEP

1 Punch three holes where you want the center of the flowers to be on the 3¼-inch-square (8.3 cm) card.

2 Place about 20 inches (50.8 cm) of the ribbon on the needle. Run the needle up through a punched hole, leaving a couple of inches of ribbon on the under side. On the top side of the card, loop the ribbon around where you want the petal to be and run the needle back through the center hole and then back up at the end of the petal catching the loop of ribbon as you pull the needle through.

3 Place a bead on the needle down at the end of the petal and then run the needle back through the hole. Run the needle back up through the

center hole and repeat for the four other petals. Run the needle and ribbon back up through the center, place three beads of another color on the ribbon, run the ribbon back down the center hole again, and tie a knot on the back side under the flower. Repeat steps 2 and 3 for the other two flowers.

4 Punch a hole in each corner of the card. Punch eight holes along each edge.

5 Thread 20 inches (50.8 cm) of ribbon on the needle. Run the needle and thread up through a corner hole leaving 1 inch (2.5 cm) of the ribbon on the underside.

6 Place another color bead on the ribbon and stitch down through the next hole and then

back up. Place another bead and stitch back up. When you get to the next corner, stitch down through the corner hole and then back up through the next hole and then back down the corner hole, so that ribbon comes out each side of the corner hole. Now stitch back up the second hole and place a bead on the ribbon. Stitch this way all the way around and tie a knot where you began.

7 Fold the 4 x 8-inch (10.2 x 20.3 cm) piece of card stock in half creating a 4-inch-square (10.2 cm) card with a side fold. Glue the beaded card securely in position on the center front of the folded card.

The Great Frame Up

Proudly display tiny artworks, photos, or pretty fabrics inside this card's clever frame.

Designer: **CANDIE COOPER**

MATERIALS

- Miniature frame
- Beaded trim, 3 inches (7.6 cm)
- Multi-purpose adhesive
- Scissors
- Card blanks in desired colors/patterns
- Decorative papers to match card blanks
- Glue stick
- Pencil
- Utility knife
- Hole punch (optional)
- Ribbon (optional)

■ STEP BY STEP

1 Place a line of glue on the bottom backside of the frame and adhere the beaded trim. Once the glue has dried thoroughly, you can cut away the excess trim on the sides and back.

2 Cut a piece of decorative paper to go down the middle section of the card and glue into place with the glue stick. You can add as many layers of paper as you like.

3 Center the frame on the front of the card and trace around the inside with a pencil. Cut out the rectangle shape with a utility blade.

4 Place a line of glue around the back of the frame, glue to the front of the card, and leave to dry.

5 For an extra embellishment, punch two holes at the top of the card and slide a ribbon through. The tails can be tacked in place with a touch of glue.

Beaded trim and decorative paper come in a wide variety of styles, meaning you never have to make the same card twice.

Something Blue

This vintage card is accented with tiny pearls and romantic cutouts. It's perfect for a wedding or bridal shower.

Designer: **SUSAN MOSTEK**

THE PROJECTS

MATERIALS

- 2 sheets light blue card stock
- Dark blue pigment ink
- Bride stamp
- Clear embossing powder
- Heat gun
- Color pencils
- Paper cutter (optional)
- Scissors
- 2 sheets cream card stock
- Decorative corner punch
- 2 sheets dark blue card stock
- Double-sided tape
- Industrial glue
- Pearl bridal spray
  (or 16 small pearl beads)

■ STEP BY STEP

1 Using the dark blue pigment ink, stamp the bride image onto a 3¼ x 5¼-inch (8.3 x 13.3 cm) piece of light blue card stock. Sprinkle with clear embossing powder and heat set it with a heat gun. Color the image with pencils.

2 Cut the cream card stock to 3⅝ x 5⅝ inches (9.2 x 14.3 cm). Punch all four corners with the punch. Insert the stamped image into the corners.

3 Layer the entire piece onto a slightly larger dark blue piece of card stock using the double-sided tape. Finish by layering onto a slightly larger piece of cream card stock, then a layer of light blue and finally to a 6⅞ x 4¾-inch (17.5 x 12 cm) folded dark blue card.

4 Add two pearl bridal sprays to the bride's veil with the industrial glue. Cut four pearls off the spray and affix in the same manner to each of the four corners.

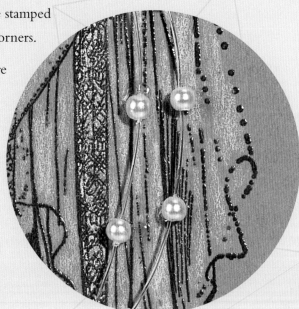

Flight of the Dragonfly

A dragonfly with shiny wings and
stunning beads takes a magical flight.

Designer: **PATRICIA DiBONA**

MATERIALS

- Double-sided tape
- Green printed paper,
  4 inches (10.2 cm) square
- Card blank, 7 x 5 inches
  (17.8 x 12.7 cm)
- Dragonfly cutout
- Adhesive glaze
- Jewelry glue
- 2 turquoise 7 mm beads
- Seed beads
- 24-gauge copper head pin,
  2 inches (5.1 cm) long
- Needle-nose pliers
- Wire cutters
- Small hole punch
- 1 mini-brad
- Glue or foam dots
- Gold metallic paint
- Paintbrush or sponge
- Gold metallic paint

■ STEP BY STEP

1 Using double-sided tape, attach the green printed square 1¾ inches (4.4 cm) from the top of the card, with equal spacing on each side.

2 Coat the dragonfly cutout with adhesive glaze and let it dry completely.

3 Glue one turquoise bead on the dragonfly's head. String the remaining turquoise bead and seed beads on the head pin and create a loop at the end with needle-nose pliers. Trim any excess with wire cutters.

4 Using the head pin as a guide, punch a small hole in the dragonfly's tail where the end loop will lie. Thread the mini-brad through the head pin loop and secure on the underside. Glue the bead string to the dragonfly body with jewelry glue.

5 Mount glue or foam dots on the back of the dragonfly and attach to the background sheet using double-sided tape.

6 Brush gold metallic paint on the right edge of the card.

119

THE PROJECTS

Mad for Monogram

Impress the recipient of this card with the luxurious simplicity of their initials monogrammed in beads.

Designer: **JOAN K. MORRIS**

MATERIALS & TOOLS

- Pencil
- Card blank, 3½ inches (8.9 cm) square
- Seed beads
- Beading needle
- Thread to match beads
- Size "E" beads
- Card stock, 4 x 8 inches (10.2 x 20.3 cm)
- Glue stick

■ STEP BY STEP

1 On a scrap piece of paper, draw out an initial. You can blow up a font from your computer or find clip art alphabet if you don't want to draw it yourself.

2 Lightly trace your letter onto the 3½-inch-square (8.9 cm) card blank. Place the letter on top of the card stock and press the pencil very hard over the letter and it will leave a mark.

3 Stitch the seed beads in place on top of the traced letter, putting the needle through the card from back to front. To keep the beads in line, place about four beads on the thread, then poke a hole from front to back, pulling the thread through. Repeat, pulling the thread back up through the previous stitch and then through the same beads again. Add four more beads and repeat.

4 On curves, you can only stitch one or two beads at a time, but keep them connected to the previous bead. Place a larger bead on ends or corners to embellish the initial.

5 Place larger beads along the edge of the card in the desired pattern.

6 Fold the 4 x 8-inch (10.2 x 20.3 cm) card stock in half creating a 4-inch-square (10.2 cm) card with a top fold.

7 Use the glue stick to glue the beaded card in place centered on the front of the folded card.

Greenwood Gem

This card depicts a simple, single iconic topiary inspired by the landscapes of American painter Grant Wood.

Designer: **ELIZABETH BECK**

MATERIALS

- Pencil
- Printed paper—a page from a novel, dictionary, map, or sheet music works well
- Acrylic paints in several shades of green
- Matte medium
- Small paintbrush
- Watercolor paper
- Scissors
- Brown permanent pen or paint
- Brown paper, or a cut-out wood image from a catalog or magazine
- Needle
- Green embroidery floss
- Beading needle
- Variety of small green beads
- Thread

■ STEP BY STEP

1 In pencil, draw a stack of circles on your printed paper.

2 Mix the dark green paints with the matte medium to make a glaze, or transparent layer of paint. Use your darkest green to paint over your pencil circles. Use a lighter green glaze to fill in the circles, overlapping the still wet darker paint, making a gradation of color from dark to light. Blot with another paper, if the glaze is not transparent enough.

3 Let the glaze dry, then cut out the topiary, using the project photo as your guide.

4 Cut your watercolor paper to the size card you want—the card shown is 6 x 4½ inches (15.2 x 11.4 cm). Paint the card thoroughly with a light green glaze. Go over it loosely with a second darker green glaze. Paint both sides of the watercolor paper if you'd like the inside of the card to be green too.

5 Draw a brown tree trunk onto the card. Use matte medium to glue the tree shape onto the trunk. Cut out the brown paper into a rectangle or planter shape. Use matte medium to glue the paper onto the card.

6 Use green embroidery floss to make a running stitch around the perimeter of the card, attaching green glass beads. Pre-poking the holes helps make the stitches straighter. With green thread, sew the smallest green beads onto the topiary.

Funky Felt Flowers

Layered felt flowers in funky colors add contrast and texture to this fun card.

Designer: **BRANDY LOGAN**

MATERIALS

- 3 large felt flowers
- 3 medium felt flowers
- 3 small felt flowers
- Needle and thread
- 3 small metallic flower beads
- Brown card stock,
  4¼ x 6½ inches (1.8 x 16.5 cm)
- Craft glue
- Pink card stock,
  4¾ x 9½ inches (12 x 24.1 cm)
- Bone folder
- Glue stick

■ STEP BY STEP

1 Make three flower arrangements by layering the biggest flowers on the bottom and the smallest flowers on top. You can cut out the flowers from felt yourself or buy them precut.

2 Sew one small flower bead onto the center of each flower arrangement.

3 Glue your flowers horizontally across the bottom of the brown card stock with craft glue.

4 Fold pink card stock in half, smooth with the bone folder, and glue brown card stock to the front of the card.

About the Contributing Artists

Sharon Bateman is a mixed-media artist known for her magazine articles, appearances on DIY Network's *Jewelry Making*, beading books that include *Findings and Finishings* (Interweave Press, 2003), and the self-published titles *Morning Rose Rosette* (2001), *Peepers and Creepers* (2000), and *Over the Edge* (2005). She invented Sharondipity Tube Looms: plastic looms for specific projects. She can be reached at www.sharonbateman.com.

Elizabeth Beck is a mixed-media artist intrigued by collages. She makes colorful, exuberant art and wants her work to reflect happiness, using quirky ephemera in traditional compositions. Elizabeth lives in Atlanta with her husband and three children. More of her work can be seen at www.ebeckartist.blogspot.com and www.flickr.com/photos/ebeck.

Candie Cooper's passion lies in designing jewelry from unique materials and vibrant colors. She is the author of *Felted Jewelry* (Lark Books, 2007) and creator of many designs in various publications. Her jewelry has been exhibited around the world, and she works and teaches from her studio in Shenzhen, China. See more at www.candiecooper.com.

Debbie Crane is a wife, mom, and elementary art teacher in southern Indiana. She has been a serious book and paper artist since 2002, and her work has been shown in galleries around the United States, as well as published in books and magazines. More of her work can be seen at www.paperdollpost.blogspot.com.

Patricia DiBona is an award-winning artist and teacher. She owns DiBona Designs, in Alpharetta, Georgia, and through her collage and specialty papers, accordion books, and specialty embellishments, she adds a new dimension to the art of bookmaking. See her work at www.dibonadesigns.com.

Sandra Evertson of Austin, Texas, is a mischievous artist whose passion for beauty leads her to create. She has authored several books, including *Fanciful Paper Projects* (Sterling, 2005) and *Fanciful Paper Flowers* (Lark Books, 2007), been published in Stampington & Company's magazines, and served in the Director's Circle Artists for *Somerset Studio*. She contributed to the book *Romantic Homes* and was featured in *Where Women Create*.

Lisa Glicksman is a mixed-media artist with a fondness for paper arts, rubber stamping, and painting, and she looks for ways to incorporate her collections into her work. Lisa lives in Oakland, California, with her husband. Her work has exhibited locally and appeared in *Artful Paper Dolls* (Lark Books, 2006). Her website is www.glixart.com.

Kim Grant's primary mediums include acrylics, watercolors, collage, and water media. Her works have been featured in national publications, and she has written for magazines such as *Somerset Studio*, *Stampington & Company*, *Better Homes & Gardens*, and *Cloth, Paper, and Scissors*. She is a collaborative artist in two books: *Artful Paper Dolls* and *New Directions in Altered Books* (both Lark Books, 2006).

Brandy Logan lives in the mountains of North Carolina with her husband and two children. She is an avid scrapbooker and enjoys all types of paper crafting. Her work is often published on her personal blog and can be seen at www.brandylogan.blogspot.com.

Susan McBride is a designer, illustrator, and writer. She has a special interest in lino-cut art. Many of her designs have been featured in Lark Books. To see more of her work go to www.susanmcbridedesign.com.

Nicole McConville is an artist with a background in correspondence art and collage. She has made cards since she was a little girl, always preferring the handmade to the manufactured when a personal gesture is needed. You can view more of her work at www.sigilation.com.

Jean Tomaso Moore is a mixed-media artist who lives and works in Asheville, North Carolina. She has designed projects for numerous books, including *The Altered Object* and *Artful Paper Dolls* (both Lark Books, 2006). Jean can be reached at LeaningTowerArt@msn.com.

Joan K. Morris's artistic endeavors have led her down successful creative paths, including ceramics and motion picture costume design. Joan has contributed projects for numerous Lark books, including *Hardware Style*, *Hip Handbags*, *Beaded Home*, *Tops to Sew*, *Pillows to Sew*, *Curtains to Sew*, and many more.

Susan Mostek's love of rubber stamping and paper crafts developed when she moved to Boulder, Colorado, with her husband and two children. Since then she has taught a variety of paper craft techniques, and her artwork has been featured in publications including *The Stamper's Sampler* and *Rubber-StampMadness*. Susan currently works as a designer and demo artist for B-Line Designs.

Rain Newcomb has been beading since she was 15. When she's not beading or editing children's books for Lark, she's giving her poodle mohawks and other unique haircuts. She's the author of *The Girl's World Book of Jewelry*, and several other Lark books.

Jane Reeves lives in Black Mountain, North Carolina, where she makes quilts, collages, and mixed-media art. Her favorite art materials are cheesecloth and rusty nails, but she usually can't resist adding some flowers and beads to everything she makes.

Sharon Rohloff has been doodling all her life. Trained as a graphic artist, her introduction to the crafting world was as a rubber stamp artist for several companies. After moving to Boulder, Colorado, she began teaching altered book art and card making, and she enjoys combining sewing and three-dimensional elements in her artwork. Sharon is currently writing a children's book.

Carla Schauer brings eye-catching style to the creative world through her artistry. Carla began scrapbooking in 2000, and she has broadened her interests to include other paper arts. She delights in creating gifts for family and friends, as well as instructing others through classes at her local scrapbook store. Her work can be seen in a variety of magazines and books, and at www.scrapbookresumes.com/CarlaSchauer/.

Terry Taylor is the author of several Lark books. When not working on books or projects for books, he's a mixed-media artist and jeweler. He studied jewelry and metal work at John C. Campbell Folk School, Appalachian Center for Crafts, and Haystack Mountain School of Crafts.

Acknowledgments

A big thank-you card to:

• The editorial team of Ray Hemachandra, Larry Shea, Cassie Moore, Amanda Carestio, Mark Bloom, James Knight, and Terry Taylor

• The design and production team of Kristi Pfeffer, Shannon Yokeley, and Jeff Hamilton

• Photographer John Widman, cover designer Cindy LaBreacht, and proofreader Be Engler

Most of all, thanks to all the talented designers who contributed their wonderful cards to this book.

Index